THE TSARS' CABINET

TWO HUNDRED YEARS OF
RUSSIAN DECORATIVE ARTS
UNDER THE ROMANOVS

from THE KATHLEEN DURDIN COLLECTION
OF RUSSIAN DECORATIVE ARTS

with an essay by ANNE ODOM

INTERNATIONAL ARTS & ARTISTS, WASHINGTON, DC

The Tsars' Cabinet is developed from the Kathleen Durdin Collection and is organized by the Muscarelle Museum of Art at the College of William & Mary, Williamsburg, Virginia, in collaboration with International Arts & Artists, Washington, D.C.

EXHIBITION DATES
The Gardiner Museum of Ceramic Art, Toronto, Canada, October 13, 2011–January 8, 2012
Sonoma County Museum, Santa Rosa, CA, February 17, 2012–May 27, 2012
Royal Alberta Museum, Edmonton, Alberta, Canada, October 6, 2012–Janurary 2, 2013
The Cummer Museum of Art and Gardens, Jacksonville, FL, January 26, 2013–April 27, 2013
The Bowers Museum of Cultural Art, Santa Ana, CA, June 15, 2013–September 8, 2013

ISBN: 978-0-9662-8590-1
Library of Congress Control Number: 2011936854

© 2011 International Arts & Artists. All rights reserved. This book may not be reproduced without written permission from International Arts & Artists (IA&A) and the author. IA&A is a non-profit organization dedicated to increasing cross-cultural understanding and exposure to the arts internationally through exhibitions, programs and services to artists, arts institutions, and the public.

Essay Text © 2011 Anne Odom

Produced by International Arts & Artists, 9 Hillyer Court, NW, Washington, DC, 20008, www.artsandartists.org

Production Editor and Manager: Marlene Rothacker Harrison and Nicole Byers
Design: Simon Fong, International Arts & Artists' Design Studio
Photography: Giovanni Lunardi

Front cover image:	Campana Urns Illustrating the Arts, hard-paste porcelain, Imperial Porcelain Factory, Russia, c. 1845 (page 40, no. 130)
Front flap image:	Egg, hard-paste porcelain, Imperial Porcelain Factory, Russia, c. 1890 (page 44, no. 141)
Back cover and flap image:	Teapot from the Gothic Service, hard-paste porcelain, Imperial Porcelain Factory, Russia, c. 1833 (page 39, no. 113)
Frontispiece:	Miniature Vase from the Service for Grand Duke Paul, hard-paste porcelain, Königliche Porzellan-Manufaktur Berlin, Germany, c. 1775–1780 (page 33, no. 83)

This book was typeset in Garamond and Museo Sans. Printed by MOSAIC, which is 100% wind powered, carbon neutral, an EPA Green Power Partner and an EPA Climate Leader. The text pages are printed on FSC-certified 100# Sappi Galerie Silk Text. The Forest Stewardship Council (FSC) is a non-profit organization established to promote responsible management of the world's forests.

CONTENTS

8   Preface
by David Furchgott, President & CEO
International Arts & Artists

8   Dedication

9   Introduction
by Aaron H. De Groft, Ph.D., Director
Muscarelle Museum of Art

11   Russian Porcelain: Symbols of Power and Identity
by Anne Odom, Curator Emeritus
Hillwood Museum and Gardens

     11   The Role of Porcelain and Dining in Eighteenth Century Russia
     12   Early Attempts to Produce Porcelain in Russia
     13   Catherine and the Politics of Porcelain
     17   Alexander I and Nicholas I: Expressions of Russian Nationalism
     21   Alexander II to the End of the Empire: Porcelain's Reduced Role
     56   Bibliography

22   Catalogue

57   Glossary

57   Biography: Kathleen Durdin

PREFACE

It has been a great pleasure to collaborate once again with the Muscarelle Museum of Art at the College of William & Mary on *The Tsars' Cabinet* exhibition. This renowned collection of Imperial Russian porcelian and decorative arts is among the finest to exclusively tour museums in North America. The Muscarelle Museum of Art took great care in selecting the objects for the initial exhibition of the *The Tsars' Cabinet* at their own institution in 2006 by highlighting the production of craftsmen and artists under the Romanovs. We are deeply indebted to Dr. Aaron De Groft, who brought us the idea for this exhibition to tour and organized the collaboration among International Arts & Artists, the Muscarelle, and Kathleen Durdin.

We appreciate Kathleen Durdin's ardent efforts as collector of *The Tsars' Cabinet*. We are also honored to have Anne Odom, curator emeritus, at Hillwood Museum and Gardens in Washington, D.C., contribute her fascinating essay which takes the reader on a journey through Russian decorative arts styles during the period of Romanovs, directly reflecting the history of the country. This exhibition is a rare opportunity to have two hundred years of precious, rarely-seen works in one exhibition.

Within IA&A, we acknowledge the assistance of the director of our Traveling Exhibitions Service, Marlene Rothacker Harrison; Nicole Byers, the senior exhibitions manager who managed the tour; Elizabeth Wilson, assistant director and head registrar, and Dana Thompson, registrar, for organizing the loans. We also thank Allison Keilman, venue coordinator, for her diligent work in preparing materials for the venues, and Simon Fong, IA&A's Design Studio director and designer of this catalogue.

For the benefit of all,
David Furchgott
President & CEO
International Arts & Artists

DEDICATION

This book is dedicated to Anne Curtis Odom (1935–2011). As this publication was being finalized, Ms. Odom tragically passed away. Curator Emeritus at the Hillwood Estate Museum and Gardens in Washington, D.C., she was the foremost scholar and curator of Russian arts, and gave generously of her time and vast knowledge to her many friends and colleagues, as well as contributing an essay to this publication. She is known for authoring important books on Imperial porcelain, silver and decorative arts including *A Taste for Splendor: Russian Imperial and European Treasures from the Hillwood Museum*, *Russian Enamels* and *Russian Silver in America: Surviving the Melting Pot*. She will be greatly missed by all.

INTRODUCTION

The Tsars' Cabinet illustrates two hundred years of decorative arts of Russia from the time of Peter the Great in the early eighteenth century to that of Nicholas II in the early twentieth century. Many of the pieces in the exhibition were designed for the use of the tsars or other Romanovs. Others are indicative of the styles that were prominent during their reigns. While many are in forms to be used everyday, they demonstrate the richness of Russia during the long reign of the Romanovs.

The items included in this exhibition not only trace the history of the Romanovs, but also provide the context for their reigns. Russian style during the eighteenth and nineteenth centuries reflected the history of the country. Through these items, we see the tension between the desire to be part of Europe and the fascination with an earlier Russia. Styles from the eras of specific tsars show what was important during those periods—from the Enlightenment under Catherine the Great to the militarism of Nicholas I in the mid nineteenth century. The items in this exhibition demonstrate the creativity of the artists and artisans who created the items. The artists' accomplishments can be seen in the beauty of their creations. The items in this exhibition also provide a glimpse into the everyday lives of tsars and their court. In so doing, they capture our imagination and fascination.

Decorative arts reflect the period in which they were created and the use to which the objects were put. The term "decorative arts" refers to the artistic application to the surface of useful objects. These objects can include buildings, interiors of rooms as well as small useful objects, such as those in the exhibition. Decorative arts illustrate the styles prevalent during a time through the objects people use. When they are made with rare or precious materials or with innovative stylistic approaches, they are works of art.

The Muscarelle Museum of Art at the College of William & Mary, the second oldest college in our nation and oldest university, is honored to organize and tour with the international exhibitions firm, International Arts & Artists, an exhibition of such a high quality and profoundly important group of works. It is important to recognize Kathleen Durdin for sharing her wonderful works that once graced the tables and private rooms of the royalty of Russia. I must thank Giovanni Lunardi and Lunardi Photography for so capturing the elegance and beauty of these works of art.

Aaron H. De Groft, Ph.D.
Director
Muscarelle Museum of Art

RUSSIAN PORCELAIN: SYMBOLS OF POWER AND IDENTITY[1]

by Anne Odom, Curator Emeritus
Hillwood Museum and Gardens

The discovery of the recipe for making hard paste porcelain in Europe in 1709 coincided with rapid changes in the ceremony of dining that had begun in the court of Louis XIV in France. Initially the services used on the table for royal banquets were composed of silver, whose shapes and forms expanded as French tastes demanded a growing number and variety of foods and dishes. Ceramics, whether local faience or finer Chinese and Japanese porcelains, were used in the seventeenth and early eighteenth centuries, primarily for dessert. The latter, however, were expensive and costly to import. Nevertheless these imported wares tempted European royalty to fund the search for the secret to making this fine porcelain in their own countries. Following the success of Johann Friedrich Böttger at Meissen in Saxony, other courts gradually developed their own recipes, despite Saxony's Draconian security measures to protect them. The court of Elizabeth I of Russia (r. 1741–1761) was not to be outdone. In 1744, Elizabeth founded a porcelain factory and two years later in 1746, a young chemist Dmitrii Vinogradov, who had studied metallurgy at the University of Marburg in Germany, successfully developed the body of real porcelain, which contained kaolin and petuntse.

Ceremonial dining according to the rituals established by Louis XIV spread across Europe to every court, regardless of size. It was on the occasions of dynastic marriages, coronations, military victories, and diplomatic exchanges that royalty would prepare grand banquets to augment triumphal arches, illuminations, and fireworks.[2] For such occasions, emissaries and relatives from all over Europe could be counted on to be in attendance. Thus, these events presented a special opportunity for the host ruler to demonstrate his refined tastes and the brilliance of his native artisans. The visitors in attendance served the same role as modern media spreading word of the latest cultural fashion far and wide. Because of the special value of porcelain in the eighteenth century, it early became a highly prized gift on such occasions as well. A royal palace furnished in the latest style, extensive gardens surrounding it, as well as a luxurious banqueting table all worked to create a lasting impression on the visitor. Existing descriptions of banquets and the surviving porcelain used at them are just small indicators of what the rulers thought about themselves and the unique aspects of their country, what one author has referred to it as "a theater of self-presentation."[3]

THE ROLE OF PORCELAIN AND DINING IN EIGHTEENTH-CENTURY RUSSIA

Dining during the reign of Catherine attained a level of splendor unseen in Russia before or after. Russian dining mirrored European customs. Russians had hired French chefs to prepare new dishes and silversmiths and porcelain makers copied French tureens, monteiths, sauce boats, and other serving wares. Russians were famous for huge quantities of food, offering a large number of dishes in each course—two soups, one hot, one cold, fish, meat, fowl, and several desserts.[4] Russian dining required a large number of plates because clean ones were provided for each dish. This quantity overwhelmed foreigners. Martha Wilmot, who lived with Princess Ekaterina Dashkova for about six years in the early nineteenth century at her estate outside Moscow, complained about this in letters home to Ireland. Tired from being "offer'd fifty or sixty different Dishes by servants who come one after another and flourish ready carv'd fish, flesh, fowl, vegetables, fruits, soups of fish, etc., etc. before your eyes, wines, Liqueures [sic!], etc. etc. in their turn. Seriously the profusion is beyond anything I ever saw."[5]

It should be noted in this context that Catherine was not particularly interested in food herself. Instead she devoted attention to what it was served in, the message it might send, and in the conversation at the table. The Russians took special pride in putting

◀ **Porcelain figure of Vodonoska, The Water Carrier**, hard-paste porcelain, Imperial Porcelain Factory, Russia, c. 1817. The well-known figure of the water carrier was first modeled by sculptor Stepan Pimenov as part of the Guriev Service (*page 35, no. 96*).

Snuffbox, hard-paste porcelain, Imperial Porcelain Factory, unmarked, Russia, c. 1755 (*page 25, no. 10*).

Figure of Justice from Dowry Service, porcelain bisque, Imperial Porcelain Factory, Russia, c. 1796 (*page 28, no. 31*).

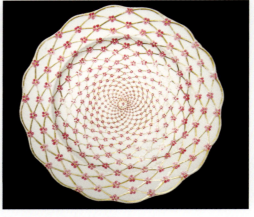

Plate from Her Majesty's Own Service, hard-paste porcelain, Imperial Porcelain Factory, Russia, c. 1756 (*page 26, no. 16*).

out of season fruits on the table, either by having them delivered by messenger from southern climes or raising them in their hothouses.[6] Martha Wilmot also commented on fruits, saying "Dinners that end after four hours uninterrupted Cramming of every delicacy that Nature and Art can procure—Grapes freshly gather'd, Pineapples, ditto, asparagus ditto, besides fruit preserved with such care that there is a Stout battle between Nature and the Cook for which is genuine, Peach, plumb, etc. etc. etc."[7] This passion for fresh fruit explains the appearance of fruit baskets in all the early services.

In Russia, as in the rest of Europe, dessert was the *pièce de résistance*. Here porcelain reached its creative apogee. Often the table was cleared and reset for dessert or dessert was served in another room. A special centerpiece (a *surtout d'table*) or in Russian, a *file*, (pronounced filet) filled the center of the dessert table. It usually related to a theme of gardens, one taken from mythology, or various allegories. Such scenes were a combination of architectural details together with figures from the *Commedia dell-Arte*, or shepherds and shepherdesses, gods and goddesses, allegorical figures, Oriental figures, and tradesmen. These sculptures were the successors to the sugar ornaments, which have been traced back to eleventh-century Egypt.[8]

EARLY ATTEMPTS TO PRODUCE PORCELAIN IN RUSSIA

Peter the Great (r. 1682–1725) probably first saw examples of Asian porcelains in Berlin on his Grand Tour of 1697–1698, when he travelled through Prussia to Holland. In his small pavilion, Mon Plaisir at Peterhof, he created a porcelain cabinet with lacquered walls. As with many other of the arts he wished to see developed in Russia, Peter sent artisans to Amsterdam to learn the art of porcelain making, but his efforts were unsuccessful. His niece Anna (r. 1730–1740) sent caravans to China, not only to bring back porcelains, but also instructing her emissaries to discover the recipe to hard-paste porcelain. Her efforts also failed.

It thus fell to Elizabeth (r. 1741–1761) to fulfill her father's dream by establishing a porcelain factory in 1744. In 1745, Elizabeth received from Augustus III Elector of Saxony a Meissen dessert service on the occasion of the marriage of her nephew Peter (later Peter III) to Princess Sophia of Anhalt-Zerbst (the future Catherine the Great). This service is decorated with the Russian double-headed eagle and the Cross of St. Andrew alternating with flowers. This was the largest service made at Meissen to that date to be sent to any court.[9] Thus began the use at the Russian court of special dessert services for the banquets honoring the knights of Russia's principle orders, in this case, the Order of St. Andrew First Called.

Vinogradov had not yet been successful in his pursuit of the right chemical mix when Elizabeth received the St. Andrew Service. The first objects he produced were small and the quality uneven as Vinogradov experimented with different ingredients in the composition of the paste. But by 1756, he had built a kiln large enough to fire baskets and platters, and Her Majesty's Own Service (*Sobstvennyi*), a dessert service, was the first to be made at the factory. It should be noted that services, understood as a matching set of silver or porcelain, evolved slowly in the eighteenth century. Initially not all pieces used for different courses shared the same ornament. The first porcelain "services" were for dessert or for coffee and tea.

Plate from the Orlov Service, hard-paste porcelain, Imperial Porcelain Factory, Russia, 1765-1770 (*page 26, no. 19*).

Figure of Cossack Woman, **Figure of Cossack Man**, and **Figure of Tartar Woman**, 1785–1800, Imperial Porcelain Factory, Russia (*pages 30–31, nos. 57, 58 & 48*).

CATHERINE AND THE POLITICS OF PORCELAIN

By the end of Elizabeth's reign in 1761, the factory was firmly grounded and was able to survive a period of inattention during the early years of Catherine's reign. It was only in 1765 that Catherine ordered a reorganization of the factory and began to give it the attention she gave to all of Russia's luxury industries. The quality of the paste and the decoration soon improved dramatically, as did the growing quantity of production.

Catherine was always lavish in the gifts she presented to her servitors, lovers, and diplomats. As an example, she presented silver services in 1765 to thirty-three of her major supporters on the third anniversary of the coup that placed her on the throne. She especially rewarded Grigorii Orlov, her favorite, with a porcelain toilet and breakfast service. The dates of production of this service are unclear, but it appears to have been produced in two parts. The tea service and plates have as their only decoration Orlov's initials GGO in Cyrillic in gold within a wreath of laurel leaves, with flags, banners, and cannon in silver to the side. Tenting scenes encircle the cups and the rims of the plates. It is thought that the service was presented in 1765 when Orlov was promoted to the rank of Chief of Artillery. A second part of the service, which included a mirror and utensils for shaving and even dental tools, is more neoclassical in design, and the military scenes are painted in polychrome. Gavrill Kozlov, a professor at the Academy of Arts designed this part of the service.

In 1772, Frederick the Great presented Catherine with a dessert service made in Berlin to commemorate the Prussian-Russian alliance concluded in 1770.

It was one of the largest made at the Königliche Porzellan Manufaktur or KPM, and Catherine exhibited it to her Chamberlain Prince Nikolai Golitsyn and Count Grigorii Orlov and other guests on August 3, 1772.[10] It is in the creations for the dessert table that the designers directed their greatest attention. The dessert centerpiece consisted of a sculptural figure of Catherine herself enthroned under a canopy with her subjects paying homage to her at the sides. Additional allegorical groups included female figures representing the arts, music, and sculpture. Another comprised the defenders of the empire, Russians and ethnic groups in authentic costume. The native types were derived from drawings by Leonard Euler, a German mathematician working at the Academy of Sciences. In 1745, he had participated in an Academy project of compiling the *Atlas of the Russian Empire*. Some of the peasants and Cossacks carry turbans signifying their triumph over the Turks who are depicted in groups bound in chains. Several political messages were tied up in this arrangement of figures. One was to display to the guest the extent of Catherine's empire and the variety of ethnic groups it included. Another was to recognize her victory over the Turks. Catherine was so pleased that she placed it on view in her Hermitage and took her guests there to drink coffee and to admire it.[11] Such gifts certainly inspired future production at the Imperial Factory.

Evidence of the impact of the Berlin porcelain figures can be seen in a series of Russian native types made at the Imperial Factory. Jean-Dominique Rachette, professor of sculpture at the Academy of Arts and head of the sculpture workshop at the Imperial Factory, created the models for these figures. They were produced between 1779 and 1809. The models were based on illustrations in a book by the German ethnographer Johann Georgi, titled *Beschreibung aller*

Cup from the Cameo Service, soft-paste porcelain, Sèvres Porcelain Manufactory, France, c. 1780. Catherine the Great commissioned the Sèvres Porcelain Manufactory to make a service for General Grigorii Potemkin. This was the most elaborate service made by the Sèvres Factory up to that time (*page 27, no. 25*).

Arabesque Service Fruit Cooler, hard-paste porcelain, Imperial Porcelain Factory, Russia, c. 1784. The Arabesque Service was the first full porcelain service produced by the Imperial Porcelain Factory (*page 27, no. 30*).

Nationen des Russischen Reiches (A Description of All People Inhabiting the Russian Empire), published in Russia in 1776. Georgi had accompanied several expeditions to the Russian interior.

There is sadly no documentation remaining about the figures, but they were surely intended as part of a centerpiece and very likely they were additions to the Berlin centerpiece. Scientists who had traveled on such expeditions were invited to dine at court, and they delighted their companions and the empress with their tales of the exotic inhabitants of this vast land.[12] Russian ethnic figures continued to be presented as gifts to foreign diplomats or other European royalty.[13] Rachette also designed a series of tradesmen and artisans. The Francis Gardner Factory, in the village of Verbilki north of Moscow, produced similar sculptures of the peoples of Russia in the second half of the nineteenth century. By then such figures, had of course, long gone out of fashion as sculptures for the table, and had become purely cabinet pieces. At the beginning of the twentieth century the Imperial Factory would introduce yet another series.[14] These figures were part of a constant quest to define national identity in this vast empire.

A centerpiece of a new type was introduced to the Russian court with the arrival of the Cameo Service, commissioned by Catherine in 1777. Catherine, who was passionate about cameos and had a large personal collection of them, sent her instructions to Prince Ivan Bariatinskii, the Russian ambassador to Versailles. The service was to be "in the newest and best style…after models taken from the Antique with cameo reproductions."[15] It was both a full dinner and dessert service.

The dessert centerpiece featured the "Russian Parnassus" with Minerva, goddess of wisdom on a pedestal surrounded by the Muses, a reference to Catherine's own wisdom, virtue and judgment. There were thirty-eight additional groups of stock sculptures, based on the theme of science and art. Unlike the Russian table figures, these were of biscuit porcelain and were considerably larger. They soon led to the production of similar figures at the Imperial Factory. Nicholas I ordered additions to this service to be made at the Imperial Factory in 1841.

This service certainly inspired Russia's first large banquet service, the Arabesque Service with sixty place settings and 973 pieces. The neoclassical design was taken from wall ornament found in the recently discovered cities of Pompeii and Herculaneum. Catherine had become impassioned with this new style, which had been introduced to her by Giacomo Quarenghi and Charles Cameron, two architects who came to work for her in the 1780s. Aleksandr Viazemskii, the Procurator General, who was also the director of the Imperial Factory together with the approval of the Academy of Arts, proposed the idea for the service.[16] Viazemskii and other advisors believed that this service would impress future generations of Catherine's contributions to Russia.[17]

The central sculpture depicts Catherine in classical dress raised on a pedestal with the orb in one hand, her scepter in the other. Her crown and the laws promulgated by her are at her side. The groups are a juxtaposition of allegorical figures representing military might and a peaceful reign. One group symbolizes Georgia under the protection of Russia and another the Crimea under Russian rule. Amphitrite represents sea power and other figures are allegories of justice and philanthropy. The apotheosis of Catherine's reign, this service was a worthy adornment of the imperial table and a testament to the quality of work at the Imperial Factory. It portrayed the empress as "the epitome of the virtues."[18] From the Renaissance to the eighteenth century, female sovereigns, especially those whose claims to the throne were uncertain, used such classical symbolism to strengthen their legitimacy.[19] Thus the centerpiece for the dessert table was not a garden display as it would have been in the time of Elizabeth, but referenced the Enlightenment. Catherine displayed the newly completed service in the Winter Palace the day after the twenty-second anniversary of her coronation, a reminder that she had fulfilled her obligations to her people.[20] In a typical entry in the *Kamerfur'erskii tseremonial'nyi zhurnal*, the official journal of what the tsar did each day, it is noted that at a dinner in June, 1799 for 125 people the table was set "with Japanese and arabesque porcelain with the gilded dishes and the Orlov Service [the silver Orlov Service] as usual for the hot course."[21] This reveals another aspect of imperial dining. Various services were used together and usually silver services for the main courses.

Closely related to the Arabesque Service, both in theme and ornament, is the Yacht Service, the first of many yacht services. The principle difference between the decoration of the two services is the central medallion. Whereas the medallions from the Arabesque Service framed allegorical groups *en camaieu* of the arts and sciences, the flag of the merchant marine is the featured motif on the Yacht Service. Questions about the origin of the service, for which no records exist, have persisted for a long time. It would appear that Catherine commissioned this service either for her famous trip to the Crimea in 1787, or immediately upon her return."[22]

The merchant flag surely alludes to the prospect of increased commerce which the acquisition of the Black Sea ports promised, and which was the purpose of this trip. It was to honor peaceful trade. The Yacht Service can also be seen as an addition to the Arabesque Service. Not only could it be used interchangeably with that service, but it extended the theme of the powerful Catherine into the realm of commerce and new lands in the South. These two services are a good example of the way that porcelain could convey political messages and complement the themes evoked by poetry written or plays produced for a given occasion. Such overt political displays were especially typical of Catherine's reign. Eighteenth-century diners were completely familiar with classical symbolism and would have understood any allegorical references.

Oval Covered Serving Dish from the Yacht Service, hard-paste porcelain, Imperial Porcelain Factory, Russia, c. 1785 (*page 28, no. 32*).

Among the most important annual banquets held at court were those honoring the knights of the orders of St. Andrew First Called, St. George the Victorious, St. Aleksandr Nevskii, and St. Vladimir, Equal to the Apostles. Catherine was not to forget the role the guards' regiments had played in her accession to the throne and thus paid close attention to the details of these ceremonies. In 1777, she commissioned dessert services for the first of the three orders from the Francis Gardner Factory. In 1782, after she had founded the Order of St. Vladimir, she ordered a fourth. This was the most important commission ever given a private factory and certainly helped propel the factory, founded by an Englishman, into the lead among the private factories for the next century.

Basket from the Service for the Order of St. Andrew First Called, hard-paste porcelain, Gardner Factory, Russia, c. 1780 (*page 31, no. 62*).

(Detail) Reticulated Basket from an Everyday Service, hard-paste porcelain, Imperial Porcelain Factory, Russia, 1780–1796 (*page 28, no. 33*).

Sauce Boat from an Everyday Service, hard-paste porcelain, Imperial Porcelain Factory, Russia, 1780–1796. (*page 28, no. 34*).

Each service included plates, round and long leaf-shaped dishes, and baskets of various sizes for fruit and a variety of ice cream and custard cups. Russians were long-time consumers of ices and ice creams, and cups for such are found in all the banqueting services. Each piece is decorated with the order's star and ribbon. In the case of the Order of St. Andrew, the chain of the order replaces the ribbon. The leaf-shaped dishes were partially molded with realistic veins running through them and natural color variations. As models for these dishes Catherine provided the designer, Gavrill Kozlov, with similar dishes from the KPM gift from Frederick the Great.[23]

Such order services are rare in the history of European porcelain, and never played the role in royal dining that they did in Russia where the appropriate service was used whenever the saints' day of the order was feted, even if the ceremony was held at one of the suburban palaces. The order services were used for dessert until the reign of Alexander II. This is evident in a note in the court record of Emperor Paul's daily activities for the Order of St. Aleksandr Nevskii banquet in 1797 held at Gatchina, Paul's favorite palace: "The table was served with the Orlov [silver] and Gatchina Services, but for dessert the order plates were used."[24] In 1856, shortly after coming to the throne, Alexander commissioned from the Imperial Factory additions for all four services. They were enlarged at this time to include candelabra.

Banqueting services were used specifically for large ceremonial occasions, otherwise the "everyday" services (*vsednevnyi*) or "ordinary" (*ordinarnyi*) were used. These were all similar; some had a molded basket-weave rim, others had a plain rim, but all were decorated with so-called "Deutsche Blumen," (German flowers), or sprays of flowers, particularly roses. In 1838, Nicholas I ordered white services, each decorated with the black double-headed eagle, as everyday ware for all of the palaces.[25]

In 1793, Catherine commissioned another large service, now known as the Cabinet Service, for her chief minister Aleksandr Bezborodko.[26] Numbering more than 900 pieces, this service is distinguished by small Italianate landscapes in medallions on a white ground. Such scenes are featured not only on this service, but also on the dowry services of all four of Catherine's granddaughters. We know now that such scenes were copied from volumes like Jean Claude Richard D. Saint-Non's *Voyage Pitoresque, Ou Description des Royaumes de Naples et di Sicile* and others. Such volumes, and there were at least two others, were compilations of engravings by different artists.[27] These views may have been used to stimulate conversation at the table about the classical monuments of antiquity. They were also a nostalgic reminder for those who had gone on the Grand Tour.

What distinguishes the Cabinet Service from ones made for Catherine's son, Emperor Paul (r. 1796–1801), and the four dowry services is their borders. The border for the Cabinet Service is painted with field flowers on a gold ground. Three of the dowry services had rims composed of roses in different arrangements. The one Paul ordered for himself is decorated on the rim with a Greek key and yet another service made for Prince Nikolai Iusupov is enlivened with a gilded scroll on a black ground. All of these services had large centerpieces composed of mythological themes for the dessert table. Maria Fedorovna, following Catherine's lead, was determined that her daughters would be provided with elaborate dowries to spread the extent of Russia's craftsmanship and artistry.

ALEXANDER I AND NICHOLAS I: EXPRESSIONS OF RUSSIAN NATIONALISM

The role of porcelain as a vehicle to convey political messages continued into the reigns of Alexander I (r. 1801–1825) and Nicholas I (r. 1825–1855). In 1809, Alexander, Catherine's grandson, commissioned the Guriev Service, one of the grandest ever produced at the Imperial Factory and certainly the largest. Originally known as "the service with illustrations of Russian costumes" or "the Russian Service," it was later named after Count Dmitrii Guriev, the director of the factory during Alexander's reign. Tureens and ice pails were painted with architectural views of St. Petersburg and its environs. Dessert plates featured ethnic types, tradesman, and artisans, derived from various sources. The images reproduced on individual pieces of the Guriev Service represent a culmination of several forces at the factory in the first decade of the nineteenth century. For the first time views of palaces and other monuments of St. Petersburg replaced the Italianate scenes that had been so popular on the Cabinet Service and its variants. The painting of recognizable cityscapes, known as *prospektmalerei* or *veduta esata*, was especially popular in Berlin and Vienna.[28] Russians had finally come to appreciate the beauty of their capital city, now one hundred years old. That the Russians began to paint their own cityscapes shows their enormous pride in what they had created. This service marks the first extensive use of Russian buildings and people as worthy subjects for art. From this time forward Russian artists more frequently searched their own culture for inspiration. This ultimately resulted in the flowering of a Russian revival movement in the last quarter of the nineteenth century.

Pair of Wine Coolers from the Dowry service of Maria Pavlovna, hard-paste porcelain, Imperial Porcelain Factory, Russia, c. 1800 (*page 32, nos. 77 & 78*).

◀ **(Handle Detail) Wine Cooler from the Dowry service of Maria Pavlovna**, hard-paste porcelain, Imperial Porcelain Factory, Russia, c. 1800 (*page 32, nos. 77 & 78*).

◀ **Square Dish from the Cabinet Service**, hard-paste porcelain, Imperial Porcelain Factory, Russia, c. 1800. The cavetto is painted with "vue site pittoresque et des Debrie de l'antique/ Theatre de Syracuse" as inscribed in overglaze black on the reverse. The Cabinet Service was ordered for Count Aleksandr Bezborodko in 1793. It reverted to the crown upon his death in 1799, and may have then become known as the "Cabinet" Service (*page 32, no. 80*).

The national pride that Russians felt about their capital was reinforced by the defeat of Napoleon and the victorious Russian army's entry into Paris in 1814. Russia had led the attack that drove Napoleon back, and Alexander was a central player at the Congress of Vienna in 1815. This confidence is reflected not only in the *veduta* paintings on porcelain, but also in the plates with military figures in the uniforms of their various regiments. The fashion for producing such dessert services seems to have started in Berlin, with the service that Friedrich Wilhelm III of Prussia presented to the Duke of Wellington in 1817. The first series of Russian plates was made during Alexander's reign, but they became

especially popular during the reign of Nicholas I (r. 1825–1855). To keep up with uniform changes, future tsars continued to commission new military plates.

Also a fitting celebration of Russia's power and prestige following the Napoleonic Wars is the service Nicholas I ordered for his coronation in 1826. The imperial coat-or-arms—the double-headed eagle, encircled by the Chain of St. Andrew, placed on an ermine mantel and surmounted by the imperial crown—is the featured motif in the center of the plate. Helmets, trophies, and lion masks decorate the rims of the dinner plates, and griffins, the symbol of the Romanov family, and wreaths are found on the dessert plates. All are rendered in tooled gold on a cobalt blue ground. The service owes a stylistic debt to the late empire style of the preceding decade. This service was made terribly quickly, probably on old unmarked porcelain from the Alexander I period. Nicholas was crowned only nine months after he came to the throne and may not have even had time to have his mark placed on the porcelain.

At Nicholas' coronation the service was actually used on the emperor's table, which was set on a dais at the end of the main reception hall in the Terem Palace in the Kremlin. Others ate from silver plates from the storeroom of the Kremlin.[29] A review of the descriptions of each coronation, from Nicholas I to Nicholas II, found in the *Kamerfur'erskii tseremonial'nyi zhurnal'* reveals that the service was never used again at the coronation day banquet, and it seems to have been returned to storage in the Winter Palace.

More frequently used at coronations was another service also commissioned by Nicholas I, known as the Kremlin Service. When he ordered this service in 1837, Nicholas introduced a rich source of decoration into Russia's vocabulary of ornament. For the first time artists drew on Old Russian motifs from the seventeenth century, dating to a period before Peter came to the throne. Believing that Russian sixteenth and seventeenth century works of art were a legitimate source of artistic inspiration, Nicholas in 1830 sponsored Fedor Solntsev, a young graduate of the Academy of Arts, in a project that was to have a major impact on the decoration arts for the rest of the century. Solntsev's task was to copy the treasures in the Kremlin Armory and wall ornament from various churches throughout Russia. Nicholas was so pleased with the results that he immediately commissioned Solntsev to provide drawings for the restoration of the old Terem Palace in the Kremlin and to design a large banquet service.[30]

The Kremlin Service was intended for five hundred people, with two thousand dinner plates, one thousand soup plates, and one thousand dessert plates.[31] The service took a long time to finish; the painting of the

Plate from the Guriev Service, hard-paste porcelain, Imperial Porcelain Factory, Russia, c. 1815. This plate has a cavetto scene of a street vendor selling *blinchicki* or pancakes to a workman carrying a ladder (*page 35, no. 91*).

Salt from the Guriev Service, hard-paste porcelain, Imperial Porcelain Factory, Russia, c. 1902 (*page 35, no. 94*).

Charger, Cup and Saucer, and Bowl from the Kremlin Service, hard-paste porcelain, Imperial Porcelain Factory, Russia, c. 1840–1855. The charger and bowl are marked with the cipher of Nicholas I and also has a Kremlin inventory number in overglaze red. The design by Fedor Solntsev (1801–1892) is based on a Turkish washbasin made for Tsarina Natalya Naryshkina (*page 39, nos. 115, 117 & 118*).

Military Plate, hard-paste porcelain, Imperial Porcelain Factory, Russia, 1836. The base is inscribed "Soldat des Comp. d'Invalides de la Garde," signed by S. Daladugin (painter), and dated 1836 (*page 37, no. 100*).

Detail of Soup Tureen from the Service for Grand Duke Konstantin Nikolaevich, hard-paste porcelain, Imperial Porcelain Factory, Russia. The finial of the tureen lid was modeled after Tsar Alexei Mikhailovich's (1629–1676) gold helmet (*page 39, no. 121*).

Dessert Plate from the Gothic Cottage Dessert Service, hard-paste porcelain, Imperial Porcelain Factory, Russia, c. 1885. In 1831, the service for the Cottage Palace was supplemented with a group of dessert plates designed to resemble Rose windows in Gothic cathedrals, consistent with the Gothic Revival design of the Cottage Palace (*page 37, no. 106*).

dessert plates was still not completed in 1847, ten years after Nicholas' order.[32] Solntsev's design for the dessert plate derived from a gold and enamel plate made in the Kremlin Armory workshops for Peter's father, Tsar Aleksei, in 1667. Another design in this large service was drawn from a Turkish washbasin. This decoration was used on large chargers and service plates. For the so-called white service, consisting of dinner plates and soup, Solntsev created a green and orange strapwork ornament in the old style of pre-Petrine Russia.

The Kremlin Service was used not only at coronations but also at other major banquets, such as the Moscow celebration of the Tercentenary of Romanov rule in 1913, by which time it was known as the "rich [*bogatyi*] Moscow service." In fact, Nicholas II ordered additions to the service at this time.[33] The Kremlin Service linked the later tsars with their Romanov ancestors. In the troubled period following the Revolution of 1905, Nicholas II used old Russian ornament to reinforce his position as autocrat of all the Russias just as Catherine had employed classical imagery to support her claim to legitimacy.

Fedor Solntsev also designed a service for Grand Duke Konstantin Nikolaevich at the time of his marriage in 1848. The plates, although often confused with the plates from the Kremlin Service, are easily identified by the cipher of Konstantin (*VKKN* for *Velikii kniaz* [Grand Duke] Konstantin Nikolaevich) on each piece. The Imperial Factory was not an enthusiastic producer of porcelain in the Russian style. In fact, Baron Nikolai von Wolf, the last director of the factory, took a dim view of the Russian style, considering it unsuitable for porcelain.[34] In the Service for the Yacht *Derzhava*, commissioned by Alexander II in 1871, the designer Ippolit Monighetti (1819–1878) employed interlace designs of ropes and chains to form double-headed eagles and anchors as part of the decoration. In Alexander's reign (1855–1883), strap-work was also employed on large neoclassical vases exhibited at international exhibitions to give them an aura of the Russian style. This was ornament that definitely appealed to Westerners as unusual and exotic.

Nicholas I was an even greater patron of the Imperial Factory than his grandmother had been. In addition to such well-known services as the Gothic Service (1832), the Etruscan Service (1844), several yacht services, elaborate dowry services for his daughters and for his niece Ekaterina Mikhailovna, he also ordered porcelain for all his sons when they married in addition to Konstantin. Nicholas also began the practice of producing additions of many of the earlier major services, whether Russian or foreign. This practice of adding on to older services was continued

Two Plates, Soup Plate (third from the left), Dessert Plate (fourth from the left), Butter Plate (fifth from the left), and Cup and Saucer (bottom) from the Raphael Service, hard-paste porcelain, Imperial Porcelain Factory, Russia (*pages 47–48, nos. 158, 157, 159, 162 & 161*).

throughout the remainder of the empire. Thus many pieces with eighteenth- or early nineteenth-century ornament can be found with the marks of later emperors. The factory also produced in this period literally hundreds of vases of all sizes.

ALEXANDER II TO THE END OF THE EMPIRE: PORCELAIN'S REDUCED ROLE

Nicholas died in 1855. When his son Alexander II came to the throne, Russia was in serious financial trouble following its defeat in the Crimean War, which ended that year. Alexander II was neither particularly interested in porcelain nor was he willing to spend the necessary funds to upgrade the factory to the standards of the European factories of the period. Only three major banqueting services were commissioned by Alexander III (r. 1881–1894) and Nicholas II (r. 1894–1917). The Raphael Service made for the Catherine Palace at Tsarskoe Selo was started in 1883 and continued production throughout Alexander's reign. Factory artists copied the ornament from drawings of the Raphael Loggia in the Vatican. These may have been the same drawings used to decorate the Raphael Loggia ordered by Catherine for the Hermitage.

Grand ceremonial dining had declined by the end of the empire, although the court was still the most lavish in Europe. At the end of the nineteenth century receptions were held in the Concert Hall in the Winter Palace and according to Princess Catherine Radzwill, writing under the name of Count Paul Vassili, "they were never crowded, as rarely more than eight hundred invitations were issued, and the supper was served in the Nicholas Hall, a splendid apartment which was transformed into a winter garden. Each small table was laid for eight to ten people, having in the middle of it a big palm tree, at the foot of which was a parterre of roses and other flowers."[35] Serving large numbers of people at small tables began already in the time of Catherine the Great. She entertained Prince Henry of Prussia in 1770 in an oval hall with twelve alcoves representing the twelve months of the year. In each was a table for ten. Lady Londonderry, who was in St. Petersburg in the 1830s, described "a fairyland—the endless vista, the quantities of massy plate, the abundance of lovely flowers, and, to crown all, the whole having the appearance of an orangerie, the supper tables being so constituted as to let the stems of immense orange trees through so that we literally sat under their shade and perfume."[36]

Nicholas commissioned two services in the neo-rococo style (the Aleksandrinskii Turquoise and the Purple or Tsarskosel'skii services). The Aleksandrinskii was intended for the Winter Palace and the Purple Service for Tsarskoe Selo. These two services reflect the prevailing Western lifestyle and conservatism of the court. The new technique of high-fire underglaze painting, learned from Danish craftsmen, resulted in the production already in Alexander III's reign of an array of vases, often painted with scenes recalling the haunting landscapes of this northern land. These vases were probably the major contribution of the factory in its last years before the Revolution of 1917.

Russian porcelain over two centuries becomes a remarkable reflection of Russia's view of itself and of its cultural aspirations. From its ethnic figures to the military plates, from classical symbolism to the Russian style, Russian designers expressed the country's desire to Westernize, but its need for empire and "otherness." As a result Russian porcelain remains easily recognizable, and this phenomenon continues into the Soviet period after 1917.

CATALOGUE

1. **Plate, Peter the Great at Zaandam,** hard-paste porcelain, China for Export, c. 1740, 9 ¼ inches diameter. The scene is painted in the manner of the Meissen Hausmaler (house painters). In 1697–98, Peter took part in the Great Embassy, traveling to the German states, Holland, and England. While in Holland, Peter stayed at the home of a neighbor of a blacksmith he knew from Russia, and worked in a shipyard for a week. This Chinese Export plate has an illustration from the Embassy, showing Peter working at a dock at Zaandem in Holland, helping to load a ship. (not pictured)

2. **Beer Beaker,** glass, Russia, first quarter of the 18th century, 6 x 3 ¼ inches. The beaker is engraved with the Imperial Eagle on one side. (photo page 24)

3. **Plate,** hard-paste porcelain, Imperial Porcelain Factory, Russia, c. 1815–1825, unmarked, 9 ⅝ inches diameter. The cavetto is painted with a scene of a street of St. Petersburg, with the Admiralty in the background. (not pictured)

4. **Egg,** hard-paste porcelain, Imperial Porcelain Factory, Russia, c. 1830–1840, unmarked, height 3 inches. The reserves of the egg each have gold-framed panels depicting "La Bourse à Petersbourg" and "Port d'Isaac." The egg is pierced at each end for hanging and gilt metal mounted. (not pictured)

5. **Cup and Saucer,** hard-paste porcelain, P. T. Fomin Factory, Russia, c. 1830–40, cup: 2 ½ x 4 x 3 ½ inches, saucer: 5 ¾ inches diameter. The pieces are marked under the bases with overglaze brown marks. The exterior of the cup has four gilded cartouches containing Russian views, including Falconet's monument to Peter the Great. The founding of St. Petersburg was commemorated with this statue that was designed by the French sculptor Etienne Falconet that Catherine the Great had erected in 1782, "Petro Primo Catharina Secunda MDCCLXXXI," the Bronze Horseman. (not pictured)

6. **Goblet,** Goblet, glass, attributed to the Iamburg Glassworks, Russia, c. 1730–40, 6 ½ x 3 ½ inches. One side is engraved with St. George slaying the dragon within a circular cartouche and the reverse has a crowned double-headed eagle with the cipher of Empress Anna Iovanovna on its breast. (not pictured)

7. **Meissen Plate from a Service made for General Field Marshall of Empress Anna Iovanovna, Count Burchardt Christoph von Münnich, from a model by Johann Joachim Kaendler,** hard-paste porcelain, Meissen Porcelain Factory, Germany, 1738–1741, 9 ¼ inches diameter. This service was presented by the court of Saxony. Count Burchardt Christoph van Münnich was from Saxony and had been a Saxon major general before becoming Empress Anna's field marshall. This service was ordered in

1738 and delivered in 1741. The service used the forms of those in the service made for Count Alexander Joseph Sulkowski. The cavetto is painted with the van Münnich coat-of-arms, the shield centered with the Imperial Eagle and surrounded by the chain and cross of the Order of St. Andrew and the Latin motto *Obsequio et Candore* (in Obedience and Honesty), set below. (*photo page 24*)

8. **Lobed Dish from the Service for the Order of St. Andrew First Called**, hard-paste porcelain, Meissen Porcelain Factory, Germany, c. 1744, 11 inches diameter. Marked under the base with the blue crossed swords mark, "Pressnummer 22," an indistinct "r" on the foot rim and a red Hermitage inventory number G. Ch. 1584. This service was presented to Empress Elizabeth by Augustus III on the occasion of the marriage of her nephew, Tsarevich Peter Fedorovich (later Peter III) to Sophia of Anhalt-Zerbst (later Catherine II). (*photo page 24*)

9. **Double Salt, later replacement for the Meissen Order of St. Andrew Service**, hard-paste porcelain, Imperial Porcelain Factory, c. 1860, 2 ¾ x 7 ½ x 5 inches. Salt has two oval bombe wells painted with vibrant wildflowers. The sides are decorated with the Russian Imperial Eagle and the cross of the order, separated by molded, raised wildflowers. (*photo page 24*)

10. **Snuffbox**, hard-paste porcelain, Imperial Porcelain Factory, unmarked, Russia, c. 1755, 1 ½ x 3 ¼ x 2 ½ inches. The interior of the lid has a portrait of Empress Elizabeth wearing the sash of the Order of St. Andrew First Called. (*photo page 12*)

11. **Tea Pot**, hard-paste porcelain, Imperial Porcelain Factory, Russia, c. 1750, 5 x 5 x 3 inches. One side is decorated with a large gilded crowned monogram within a cartouche framed by trophies, the other with an ornate family crest. The handle is molded to resemble a branch. It is marked under the base with the black Imperial Eagle mark and impressed with the circle and dot mark. (*photo page 24*)

12. **Tea Canister**, hard-paste porcelain, Imperial Porcelain Factory, Russia, c. 1750, 5 ½ x 3 ½ inches. The four sides are decorated with pastoral views within shaped cartouches and a figural flower finial on the lid. It is marked under the base with impressed circle and arrow and the gold Imperial Eagle surrounded by a wreath. (*photo page 25*)

13. **Tea Canister**, hard-paste porcelain, Imperial Porcelain Factory, Russia, c. 1750, 5 ½ x 3 ½ inches. The four sides are finely painted with scenes of military battles within shaped, gilded cartouches. The slightly domed lid has four additional cartouches further scenes and is surmounted by a figural rose finial. It is marked under the base with impressed circle and arrow and impressed eagle marks. (*photo page 25*)

14. **Goblet**, glass, attributed to the St. Peterburg Glassworks, Russia, c. 1742–1762, 10 x 4 ½ inches. One side is engraved with a bust of Empress Elizabeth surrounded by military trophies, and the other has a crowned double-headed eagle with her initials on its breast. The sides of the goblet have baskets of flowers. (*not pictured*)

25

20 & 21

18

15. **Snuffbox with the Battle of Kunersdorf**, painted enamel, Russia, c. 1760, 1 ½ x 3 ½ x 2 ½ inches. The interior of the lid has a portrait of Empress Elizabeth. The exterior of the box has a military theme, with the lid depicting a battle scene. The battle of Kunersdorf was fought during the Seven Years War in 1759, and pitted the joint Austrian and Russian force against the Prussians, led by Frederick the Great. Count Petr Saltykov, whose name appears on the box, led the Russian army. (*not pictured*)

16. **Plate from Her Majesty's Own Service**, hard-paste porcelain, Imperial Porcelain Factory, Russia, c. 1756, 10 inches diameter. The plate is marked under base with an overglazed black Imperial Eagle. Each piece of the trellis-decorated service was molded by hand. Her Majesty's Own Service (*Sobstvennyi*) was the first dessert service produced by the factory. (*photo page 12*)

17. **Map**, hand-colored paper, England, 1756, map: 11 ¼ x 13 inches, framed: 19 ½ x 21 ½ inches. John Gibson (cartographer) map of Russia that dates from the last years of the reign of Empress Elizabeth. (*not pictured*)

18. **Soup Plate with Coat of Arms**, hard-paste porcelain, China for Export, from the Qianlong period, c. 1740, 9 inches diameter. This soup plate is part of a service produced for the parents of Sophia of Anhalt-Zerbst (later Catherine the Great) Christian August (1690–1747) and Johanna Elizabeth (1712–1760) of Holstein Gottorp. (*photo page 26*)

19. **Plate from the Orlov Service**, hard-paste porcelain, Imperial Porcelain Factory, Russia, 1765–1770, 9 ½ inches diameter. The cavetto of the plate is emblazoned with the crowned monogram of Count Grigorii Orlov within laurel and palm branches. The raised border is molded and the ciselé gilt inner band has blue pellets and a ciselé silver landscape frieze. The plate is marked with the black Imperial Eagle and No. 1. (*photo page 13*)

20 & 21. **Pair of Armorial Cache-Pots from the Service of Count Zakhar G. Chernishev**, hard-paste porcelain, Imperial Porcelain Factory, Russia, c. 1762, 5 ½ x 6 ¼ inches. The cylindrical bodies of the cache-pots have scalloped gilt rims, painted on one side with the coat of arms of Count Chernishev within an oval medallion with red border, adorned by a laurel-leaf swag and suspended by a puce ribbon from the gilt border around the rim. The reverse of the cache-pots is decorated with the same coat of arms in gilt. Both are marked under base with a black Imperial Eagle, number "7" and incised circle and arrow. (*photo page 26*)

22. **Knife, Fork and Spoon from the Catherine the Great Berlin Dessert Service**, hard-paste porcelain, Konigliche Porzellan-Manufaktur Berlin, Germany, 1770–1772, Knife: 10 ¼ inches, fork: 9 inches, spoon: 9 ¼ inches. This major service was presented by Frederick the Great to Catherine the Great. All plates and cutlery were painted by Johann-Baptist-Balthasar

Borrman with battle and military encampment scenes from the Russo-Turkish war. (*photo page 27*)

23. **Leaf-shaped Dish from the Potemkin Service**, hard-paste porcelain, Königliche Porzellan-Manufaktur Berlin, Germany, c. 1775, 2 ¼ x 10 x 8 ½ inches. This service was presented by Frederick the Great to General Grigorii Potemkin. (*not pictured*)

24. **Oval Serving Dish from the Green Frog Service**, creamware, Wedgwood, c. 1774, England, 1 ½ x 11 ½ x 8 ¾ inches. Catherine commissioned a creamware service from the Josiah Wedgwood factory in Great Britain for her Chesme Palace, at one time called La Grenouillere or Kekerekeksinen, because of its location on a frog marsh near St. Petersburg. This creamware service commissioned in 1773 was in a style typical of articles produced by Wedgwood. The "Green Frog Service" was decorated with monochrome views of England painted after engravings. The dinner service was decorated with a border of oak branches, the dessert service with a border of ivy. The green frog emblem is included on all 952 individual pieces of the service. This oval serving dish is decorated with a black enamel painted landscape, surrounded by an arch and foliate banded border, and finished with an oak leaf outer band; the top is surmounted by a shield containing a green frog. The reverse markings identify the landscape as "View at Enville, Staffordshire," with an impressed mark and numbered 311. (*photo page 27*)

25. **Cup from the Cameo Service**, soft-paste porcelain, Sèvres Porcelain Manufactory, France, c. 1780, 2 ¾ x 3 ⅝ x 2 ⅝ inches. Catherine the Great commissioned the Sèvres Porcelain Manufactory to make a service for General Grigorii Potemkin. This was the most elaborate service made by the Sèvres Factory up to that time. This cup was from the Minton Factory collection. The Minton Factory made additional items for this service in the late 19th century. (*photo page 14*)

26. **Print**, paper, France, last half of the 19th century, print: 10 x 13 ½ inches, framed 19 ½ x 24 inches. The print illustrates various pieces from the Sèvres Cameo Service. (*not pictured*)

27. **Covered Cup and Saucer**, hard-paste porcelain, Königliche Porzellan-Manufaktur Berlin, Germany, c. 1780, cup: 4 ¼ x 4 x 3 ¼ inches, saucer: 5 ½ inches diameter. The cup is painted with a portrait of Catherine the Great. (*not pictured*)

28. **Plate**, hard-paste porcelain, China for Export, c. 1770–1780, 9 ¾ inches diameter. This plate is from the second Chinese Export Service made for Catherine the Great. (*not pictured*)

29. **Goblet**, glass, attributed to the St. Petersburg Glassworks, Russia, 1775, 8 x 3 ⅝ inches. One side is engraved with a large Imperial cipher of Catherine II bracketed by the date 1775 and the reverse has a crowned Imperial Eagle with her cipher on its breast. (*not pictured*)

30. **Arabesque Service Fruit Cooler**, hard-paste porcelain, Imperial Porcelain Factory, Russia, c. 1784, 7 ¼ x 9 ½ x 7 ½ inches. The Arabesque Service was the first full porcelain service produced by the Imperial Porcelain Factory. (*photo page 14*)

31. **Figure of Justice from a Dowry Service**, porcelain bisque, Imperial Porcelain Factory, Russia, c. 1796, 10 ½ x 5 x 5 ½ inches. (*photo, page 12*)

32. **Oval Covered Serving Dish from the Yacht Service**, hard-paste porcelain, Imperial Porcelain Factory, Russia, c. 1785, 14 inches. (photos,

35, 33, 36 & 34

37

39 & 38

and purple grapes, and the upper edge finished with a thin band of gilding. The base is marked with Catherine's cipher in underglaze blue. (*photos, page 28; detail page 16*)

34. **Sauce Boat from an Everyday Service**, hard-paste porcelain, Imperial Porcelain Factory, Russia, 1780–1796, 5 ³⁄₈ x 12 x 4 ¼ inches. The base is marked with Catherine's cipher in under-glaze blue. (*photos pages 28 and 16*)

35. **Ewer from an Everyday Service**, hard-paste porcelain, Imperial Porcelain Factory, Russia, 1780–1796, 9 ½ x 6 x 4 inches. This classic form ewer is decorated with a large spray of wildflowers on each side of the body along with several smaller sprays of flowers. (*photo page 28*)

36. **Sweetmeat Dish from an Everyday Service**, hard-paste porcelain, Imperial Porcelain Factory, Russia, 1780–1796, 1 ½ x 4 ¼ x 3 inches. The interior base and exterior walls are decorated with sprays of wildflowers. The applied, branch-shaped handle is painted with green highlights and the upper edge is finished with a thin line of puce. The base is marked with Catherine's cipher in under-glaze blue. (*photo page 28*)

37. **Tête à Tête**, hard-paste porcelain, Imperial Porcelain Factory, Russia, c. 1790–1800. Dimensions: tray: 1 x 13 x 11 inches, teapot: 4 ½ x 7 x 4 ½ inches, creamer: 2 ½ x 4 ½ x 2 ½ inches, cups: 2 ½ x 3 ⁵⁄₈ x 2 ¾ inches, saucers: 5 inches diameter. The set consists of two cups and two saucers, a lidded teapot and creamer, with the original oval carrying tray. The pieces have a

33. **Reticulated Basket from an Everyday Service**, hard-paste porcelain, Imperial Porcelain Factory, Russia, 1780–1796, 5 x 11 x 9 inches. The central body of the basket has a horizontal belt of molded weaving bordered top and bottom with vine-wrapped reeding in yellow and puce. The upper and lower portions of the body are made of reticulated basketwork highlighted in light green. The handles on each end are formed as green branches with figural leaves

covered dish page 15; uncovered dish page 27)

40 & 41

43 & 42

classical form. The finial of the teapot is in the shape of a female figure seated with her legs extended. Each piece of this set is painted in two colors, cobalt blue and a brownish-purple, with the rims of each wrapped with bands of gilded arches and intertwining foliate vines. The cobalt blue color only began to be used at the factory in the 1790s. (*photo page 28*)

38. **Salt**, hard-paste porcelain, Gardner Factory, Russia, 1780s–1790s, 1 ¾ x 4 x 4 inches. The triangular-shaped salt has three classical-style legs, with molded, green painted garlands of leaves with X-shaped puce ties. The body has panels with blue, yellow and white rosettes. One side has a large oval plaque painted with a rose, surmounted by a puce ribbon tie. The base is marked with underglaze blue mark of the Gardner Factory. (*photo page 28*)

39. **Salt**, hard-paste porcelain, Gardner Factory, Russia, 1780s–1790s, 1 ¾ x 3 ¾ x 3 ¾ inches. This triangular-formed salt has three classical-style legs with three sprays of wildflowers in the top corners and three smaller sprays on the upper edges. The base is marked with the underglaze blue mark of the Gardner Factory. (*photo page 28*)

40 & 41. **Reticulated Baskets**, hard-paste porcelain, Gardner Factory, Russia, 1780s–1790s, 4 x 11 ½ x 9 ¾ inches and 4 x 12 x 9 ½ inches. Each oval-form basket has a spray of wildflowers in the cavetto, and the handles of each are adorned with applied foliate highlights. (*photo page 29*)

42. **Covered Bowl from the Count Ilia Andreevich Bezborodko Service**, hard-paste porcelain, Gardner Factory, Russia, c. 1784, 6 x 13 ⅛ x 13 ⅛ inches. The interior of the dish is emblazoned with the Count's cipher in gilded and pale blue flowers, bordered by garlands of leaves and branches and surmounted by a gilded crown above the family motto *"Labore. Et. Zelo"* (By Work and Diligence) in puce. The edge of the dish has three sprays of tiny blue flowers and a gilded rim. The cover is decorated *en suite* and has a figural rose finial with gilded highlights. (*photo page 29*)

43. **Soup Tureen from the Count Ilia Andreevich Bezborodko Service**, hard-paste porcelain, Gardner Factory, Russia,

44, 45, 49, 59, 50 & 46

47, 56, 54, 53, 55, 51 & 52

c. 1784, 10 x 13 x 12 inches. Each side is emblazoned with a crowned monogram "CIAB" and the family motto *"Labore et Zelo."* The body and lid are decorated with sprays of cornflowers and gilded highlights and borders. The base is marked with an underglaze red "G." (*photo page 29*)

44. **Figure of Woman from Kamchatka**, hard-paste porcelain, Imperial Porcelain Factory, Russia, c. 1785–1800, 8 ¼ inches height. All of the following figures (numbers 44 through 59) are from the series titled *Peoples of the Russian Empire*, modeled by Jean-Dominque Rachette (1744–1809). (*photo page 30*)

45. **Figure of Man from Kamchatka**, hard-paste porcelain, Imperial Porcelain Factory, Russia, c. 1785–1800, 8 ½ inches height. (*photo page 30*)

46. **Figure of Kabardian Man**, hard-paste porcelain, Imperial Porcelain Factory, Russia,
c. 1785–1800, 8 ½ inches height. (*photo page 30*)

47. **Figure of Teleutan Tartar Woman**, hard-paste porcelain, Imperial Porcelain Factory, Russia, c. 1785-1800, 8 ½ inches height. (*photo page 30*)

48. **Figure of Tartar Woman**, hard-paste porcelain, Imperial Porcelain Factory, Russia, c. 1785–1800, 8 ½ inches height. (*photo page 13*)

49. **Figure of Ice Vendor**, hard-paste porcelain, Imperial Porcelain Factory, Russia, c. 1785–1800, 8 inches height. (*photo page 30*)

50. **Figure of Hunter**, hard-paste porcelain, Imperial Porcelain Factory, Russia, c. 1785–1800, 8 ½ inches height. (*photo page 30*)

51. **Figure of Finnish Woman**, porcelain, Imperial Porcelain Factory, Russia, c. 1785–1800, 8 ½ inches height. (*photo page 30*)

52. **Figure of Finnish Man**, porcelain, Imperial Porcelain Factory, Russia, c. 1785–1800, 8 ½ inches height. (*photo page 30*)

53. **Figure of Samoyed Man**, hard-paste porcelain, Imperial Porcelain Factory, Russia, c. 1785–1800, 8 ¾ inches height. (*photo page 30*)

54. **Figure of Samoyed Woman**, hard-paste porcelain, Imperial Porcelain Factory, Russia, c. 1785–1800, 8 ½ inches height. (*photo page 30*)

55. **Figure of Man from Lapland**, hard-paste porcelain, Imperial Porcelain Factory, Russia, c. 1785–1800, 8 ¾ inches height. (*photo page 30*)

56. **Figure of Man from Kuril Islands**, hard-paste porcelain, Imperial Porcelain Factory, Russia, c. 1785–1800, 8 ¾ inches height. (*photo page 30*)

57. **Figure of Cossack Woman**, hard-paste porcelain, Imperial Porcelain Factory, Russia, c. 1785–1800, 9 inches height. (*photo page 13*)

58. **Figure of Cossack Man**, porcelain, Imperial Porcelain Factory, Russia, c. 1785–1800, 8 ¾ inches height. (*photo page 13*)

59. **Figure of Tradesman**, hard-paste porcelain, Imperial Porcelain Factory, Russia, c. 1785–1800, 8 ¾ inches height. (*photo page 30*)

60. **Covered Custard Cup from the Service for the Order of St. George the Victorious**, hard-paste porcelain, Gardner Factory, Russia, c. 1778, 4 x 4 ¼ x 2 ½ inches. (*not pictured*)

61. **Basket from the Service for the Order of St. George the Victorious**, hard-paste porcelain, Gardner Factory, Russia, c. 1778, 3 ¾ x 10 ¼ x 10 ½ inches. (*photo page 31*)

62. **Basket from the Service for the Order of St. Andrew First Called**, hard-paste porcelain, Gardner Factory, Russia, c. 1780, 4 x 11 x 9 ½ inches. (*photos pages 31 and 16*)

63. **Plate from the Service for the Order of St. Andrew First Called**, hard-paste porcelain, Gardner Factory, Russia, c. 1780, 10 inches diameter. (*photo page 31*)

64. **Soup Plate from the Service for the Order of St. Alexander Nevskii**, hard-paste porcelain, Gardner Factory, Russia, c. 1780, 9 inches diameter. (*not pictured*)

65. **Knife and Fork from the Service for the Order of St. Alexander Nevskii**, hard-paste porcelain and silver, Gardner Factory, Russia, c. 1780, knife: 9 ⅕ inches, fork: 8 ½ inches. (*photo page 32*)

66. **Plate from the Service for the Order of St. Vladimir**, porcelain, Gardner Factory, Russia, c. 1785, 9 inches diameter. The plate is from the collection of the niece of Ambassador Joseph Davies. (*not pictured*)

67. **Covered Two-Handled Custard Cup from the Service for the Order of St. Vladimir**, hard-paste porcelain, Gardner Factory, Russia, c. 1785, 4 ½ x 4 ½ x 2 ½ inches. (*photo page 31*)

68. **Basket from the Service for the Order of St. Vladimir**, hard-paste porcelain, Gardner Factory, Russia, c. 1785, 4 ¼ x 13 x 11 ½ inches. (*not pictured*)

69. **Nut Dish from the Order of St. Vladimir Service**, hard-paste porcelain, Gardner Factory, Russia, c. 1785, 1 ⅝ x 5 x 4 inches. (*photo page 31*)

70. **Knife and Fork from the Service for the Order of St. Vladimir**, Gardner Factory, Russia, c. 1785, knife: 9 inches, fork: 7 ¼ inches. (*photo page 32*)

71 & 72. **Two Plates from the Child Service for Grand Duke Konstantin Pavlovich**, porcelain, Imperial Porcelain Factory, Russia, c. 1780–90, 6 ½ inches and 3 ½ inches diameter. The underside of the larger plate is marked with the under-glaze blue cipher of Catherine II. The smaller plate is unmarked. (*photo page 33*)

73. **Serving Bowl from the Dowry Service of Grand Duchess Aleksandra Pavlovna**, hard-paste porcelain, Imperial Porcelain Factory, Russia, c. 1796, 2 ¼ x 9 ¼ inches. The plate is marked on the back in blue underglaze with the cipher of Catherine II and "Hospice de s: Michel" in black overglaze. The cavetto is painted with a view of the Hospice of San Michel. (*photo page 32*)

74. **Double Salt from the Dowry Service of Grand Duchess Aleksandra Pavlovna**, hard-paste porcelain, Imperial Porcelain Factory, Russia, c. 1796, 3 ½ x 5 x 3 ½ inches. The oval dish is painted with a border of single pink roses on a dark-red ground, gilt line borders and gilt wreath handle on four paw feet with a center divider. (*photo page 32*)

75. **Custard Cup from the Dowry Service of Grand Duchess Aleksandra Pavlovna**, hard-paste porcelain, Imperial Porcelain Factory, Russia, c. 1796, 2 ½ x 2 ⅜ inches. The cup is of tapering form, molded with ring handles, painted with a border of pink roses on a dark-red ground, gilt line borders. (*photo page 32*)

76. **Monteith from the Dowry Service of Grand Duchess Ekaterina Pavlovna**, later called the Württemberg Service, hard-paste porcelain, Imperial Porcelain Factory, Russia, c. 1802, 5 x 12 ¼ x 7 inches. (*photo page 33*)

77 & 78. **Pair of Wine Coolers from the Dowry service of Maria Pavlovna**, hard-paste porcelain, Imperial Porcelain Factory, Russia, c. 1800, 6 ⅞ x 9 ¾ x 7 ½ inches and 6 ¾ x 9 ½ x 7 ¼ inches. (*photo page 17*)

79. **Cup and Saucer**, hard-paste porcelain, Imperial Porcelain Factory, Russia, c. 1800, cup: 2 ¼ x 2 ½ x 2 inches, saucer: 4 ⅞ inches diameter. Both are marked under their respective bases with the cipher of Paul in underglaze blue. The saucer is painted with a scene of three soldiers conversing, and the cup has a horse-mounted soldier. Both also have gilded Imperial Eagles with gilded crossed swords and olive branches. (*not pictured*)

80. **Square Dish from the Cabinet Service**, hard-paste porcelain, Imperial Porcelain Factory, Russia, c. 1800, 9 ¾ inches. The cavetto is painted with *"vue site pittoresque et des Debrie de l'antique/Theatre de Syracuse"* as inscribed in overglaze black on the reverse. The Cabinet Service was ordered for Count Aleksandr Bezborodko in 1793. It reverted to the crown upon his death in 1799, and may have then become known as the "Cabinet" Service. (*photo page 17*)

32 THE TSARS' CABINET

76

84, 83 & 85

71 & 72

81. **Goblet**, glass, attributed to the Potemkin Glassworks, Russia, c. 1780, 9 x 4 ½ inches. One side is engraved with a large crowned Imperial cipher consisting of intertwined Cyrillic "P"s; probably for Paul Petrovich, who was the Emperor of Russia between 1796 and 1801. The other side has a crowned double-headed Imperial Eagle. (*not pictured*)

82. **Basket from the Service for Grand Duke Paul**, hard-paste porcelain, Königliche Porzellan-Manufaktur Berlin, Germany, c. 1775–1780, 3 ¾ x 11 ½ x 8 ½ inches. During his mother's reign, Grand Duke Paul was fascinated by the Prussians. In 1775, Frederick the Great presented Paul with a service from the Berlin Factory decorated with a crowned double-headed eagle holding two shields, one with the crest of the Russian Empire and the other of his paternal grandfather, Holstein-Gottorp. (*photo page 32*)

83. **Miniature Vase from the Service for Grand Duke Paul**, hard-paste porcelain, Königliche Porzellan-Manufaktur Berlin, Germany, c. 1775–1780, 4 x 2 inches. The center is decorated with a crowned double-headed eagle holding two shields, one of the Russian Empire, the other of Holstein-Gottorp. (*photo page 33*)

84. **Custard Cup from the Service for Grand Duke Paul**, hard-paste porcelain, Königliche Porzellan-Manufaktur Berlin, Germany, c. 1775–1780, 2 ½ x 3 ⅛ x 2 ⅜ inches. The center is decorated with a crowned double-headed eagle holding two shields, one of the Russian Empire, the other of Holstein-Gottorp. (*photo page 33*)

85. **Salt from the Service for Grand Duke Paul**, hard-paste porcelain, Königliche Porzellan-Manufaktur Berlin, Germany, c. 1775–1780 1 ½ x 4 ⅜ x 3 ¼ inches. The center is decorated with a crowned double-headed eagle holding two shields, one of the Russian Empire, the other of Holstein-Gottorp. (*photo page 33*)

86. **Charger with Portrait of Paul**, hard-paste porcelain, Imperial Porcelain Factory, Russia, c. 1800, 12 ¼ diameter. The cavetto is finely painted with Paul's

86 & 87

88

three-quarter length portrait in full regalia surrounded by a tooled gilded band surmounted by the Imperial Eagle of finely executed gilding against a teal ground within a wide gilded border. Portrait illustrated after one by Vladimir Borowikowski, and shows Paul as the Grand Master of a Russian Order of Malta, which was created after Napoleon captured Malta. (*photo page 34*)

87. **Plate with Portrait of Grand Duchess Natalia**, hard-paste porcelain, Imperial Porcelain Factory, Russia, c. 1796, 10 inches diameter. The cavetto of the plate is finely painted with a portrait of the future Paul I's first wife Natalia wearing the breast star and sash of the Order of St. Alexander Nevskii. Her portrait is surrounded by a band of heavy gilding over molded acanthus leaves, and the molded basket weave border of the plate is painted bright blue. (*photo page 34*)

88. **Plate from the Iusupov Service**, hard-paste porcelain, Imperial Porcelain Factory, Russia, c. 1798, 9 5/8 inches diameter. Before ascending to the throne, Paul commissioned a banquet service modeled on the Cabinet Service with Italian scenes in medallions, but with a cobalt border and gilded arabesques, which became known as the Iusupov Service. This was presented to him on Christmas Day, 1798, by Nikolai Iusupov, the manager of the Imperial Factory. The cavetto shows a view of "Place De S: Jean," as stated on the underside in black overglaze text. The border is painted with a wide band of gilded scrolling foliage over a cobalt blue ground and finished with additional gilding. (*photo page 34*)

89. **Cup and Saucer**, hard-paste porcelain, Imperial Porcelain Factory, Russia, c. 1810, cup: 2 1/2 x 2 1/2 x 2 inches, saucer: 5 3/8 inches diameter. The cup is painted with the portrait of Alexander I.

90. **Tête à Tête**, hard-paste porcelain, Imperial Porcelain Factory, Russia, c. 1815–1825, tray: 14 inches diameter, teapot: 6 x 6 1/2 x 4 1/2 inches, creamer: 5 3/4 x 5 x 3 inches, cups: 3 x 3 1/2 x 3 inches, saucers: 5 1/4 inches diameter. The tray is marked under the base with the blue cipher of Alexander I. Each piece is completely covered with gilding tooled with various neoclassical scenes. The base of the tray is painted a matte green, banded by gilding. (*photo page 35*)

91. **Plate from the Guriev Service**, hard-paste porcelain, Imperial Porcelain Factory, Russia, c. 1815, 10 inches diameter. This plate has a cavetto scene of a street vendor selling *blinchicki* or pancakes to a workman carrying a ladder. The brick red border is highlighted with gilded decoration. The reverse is inscribed in black overglaze with a description of the scene. (*photo pages 19 and 35*)

92. **Plate from the Guriev Service**, hard-paste porcelain, Imperial Porcelain Factory, Russia, c. 1815, 9 3/8 inches diameter. This plate has a cavetto scene of street singers. The brick red border is highlighted with gilded

93, 94, 95, 91 & 92

decoration. The reverse is inscribed in Russian *"Les Batelliers"* and in French *"Manf re Imper le de Russie."* (*photo page 35*)

93. **Plate from the Guriev Service**, hard-paste porcelain, Imperial Porcelain Factory, Russia, c. 1815, 9 ½ inches diameter. This plate is possibly an early experimental example for the Guriev Service, which was originally known as the Russian Service. It is painted in the cavetto with a scene titled on the reverse in French *"Fille Kalmouque."* The border is decorated with gilded foliate designs between wide-gilded bands over an exposed white paste ground. The scene is quite likely taken from Johann Gottlieb Georgi's *Folk Types of Russia* (published in Russia in 1776) or Christian Gottfried Geissler's *Petersburg Scenes and Types*. (*photo page 35*)

94. **Salt from the Guriev Service**, hard-paste porcelain, Imperial Porcelain Factory, Russia, 1902, 1 ¾ x 4 x 4 inches. This is a triangular-formed open salt from the Guriev Service, resting upon three shaped feet. The center has a deep circular well. The sides of the body are painted dark red and the top has gilded highlights and borders. The underside has gilded rays emanating from the center of the well. The feet are completely gilded. (*photo pages 19 and 35*)

95. **Charger from the Guriev Service**, hard-paste porcelain, Imperial Porcelain Factory, Russia, c. 1815, 12 inches diameter. This charger has a cavetto with a stylized gilded rosette. The

90

border is finished with classical arabesques against a brick red ground. (*photo page 35*)

96. **Porcelain figure of Vodonoska, The Water Carrier**, hard-paste porcelain, Imperial Porcelain Factory, Russia, c. 1817, 9 ½ x 8 ¼ x 3 inches. The well-known figure of the water carrier was first modeled by sculptor Stepan Pimenov as part of the Guriev Service. Realistically modeled and painted, the figure has a ciselé gilt *kokoshnik*, a traditional Russian head-dress worn by women and girls, and similar details on her blue *sarafan*, a traditional long, shapeless jumper dress, and the two detachable pails with removable lids, on a shaped circular naturalistic base. It is incised under the base "No=19" and with label "351." (*photo page 10*)

97. **Plate**, hard-paste porcelain, Iusupov Factory, Russia, 1827, 9 ¼ inches diameter. Prince Nikolai Borisovich Iusupov was an aristocrat in late 18th

and early 19th century Russia (1751–1831). During 1792, Prince Iusupov became Director General of the Imperial Porcelain Factory, a position he held until 1800. In 1814, he established a factory on his estate, Arkhangel'skoe. This factory was more like an atelier, as it imported white porcelain from other factories, which were then painted there. The items produced by the factory became gifts to members of the imperial family as well as to friends and members of the Iusupov family. Decoration included portrait miniatures, landscapes, and flowers.

The cavetto of this plate is painted with a small boat rowing in the foreground and a classical-style palace in the central portion of the scene. The cavetto is ringed with a wide band of gilding, and the border is finished with additional bands of classical-style gilding. It is marked and identified on the reverse in Cyrillic. (*photo page 36*)

98. **Plate**, hard-paste porcelain, Iusupov Factory, Russia, 1826, 9 inches diameter. The cavetto is painted with a large spray of roses taken from Pierre-Joseph Redouté's book of prints, *The Roses* and titled under the scene "*Rosien de Inde a Fleurs Presque Violettes.*" The cavetto is ringed with a wide band of gilding, and the border is finished with additional bands of classical-style gilding. It is marked on the reverse in overglaze gilding "Archangelski 1826" and an impressed, stylized letter "A." (*photo page 36*)

99. **Cup**, hard-paste porcelain, Iusupov Factory, Russia, 1824, 4 ½ x 3 ¾ x 3 ¼ inches. (*photo page 36*)

100. **Military Plate**, hard-paste porcelain, Imperial Porcelain Factory, Russia, 1836, 9 3/8

inches diameter. The base is inscribed *"Soldat des Comp. d'Invalides de la Garde,"* signed by S. Daladugin (painter), and dated 1836. (*photo page 18*)

101. **Military Plate**, hard-paste porcelain, Imperial Porcelain Factory, Russia, 1832, 9 ½ inches diameter. The reverse inscribed *"Officiers Superieur et Subalterne et sodalt du R' de la Garde Ismailofky,"* and signed by P. Schetinin (painter). (*photo page 36*)

102. **Compotier from the Coalport Service**, hard-paste porcelain, Coalport Factory, England, c. 1845, 4 ¼ x 15 ¾ x 11 ½ inches. The Coalport Service was commissioned by Queen Victoria for Emperor Nicholas I in 1845. The lobed oval body has a heavily gilt gadrooned rim and two scalloped handles. The center is adorned with the badge of the Order of St. Andrew against a white ground, framed by a wide blue border having shaped cartouches containing additional Russian orders against cream grounds. The compotier is raised on four paw feet. (*photo page 37*)

103. **Beaker**, glass, attributed to either the Imperial Glassworks or Terebenev & Co., Russia, c. 1840–1850, 3 ⅝ x 3 inches. Transfer printed with a portrait of Nicholas I. (*not pictured*)

104. **Candle Shield**, bisque porcelain and brass, Russia, c. 1850, 15 ½ x 4 ½ x 5 ¾ inches. Russian bisque porcelain candle shield is mounted to a brass stand. The shield depicts a profile portrait of Emperor Nicholas I when lit from behind. (*photo page 37*)

105. **Military Portrait Plate**, hard-paste porcelain, Imperial Porcelain Factory, Russia, 1831, 9 ⅜ inches diameter. Marked under the base. The gilded rim has ciselé Imperial eagles and shakos over crossed swords and laurel leaf sprays. The base is inscribed in Russian "Lieutenant General Nikolai Ivanovich Seliavin," signed by the artist, V. Elatevskii and dated 1831. (*photo page 39*)

106. **Vodka Glass from the Cottage Service**, glass, Imperial Glassworks, Russia, c. 1830, 3 ⅜ x 2 inches. Alexandra Fedorovna, the wife of Nicholas I, was born Princess Charlotte of Prussia. In 1829, she was honored on her birthday at a mock medieval tournament at the Neus Palais at Potsdam, known as the Magic of the White Rose (she had been called the White Rose since her childhood). Her personal emblem designed for the tournament was a blue shield with a sword, embellished with wreath of white roses and the motto "For Faith, Tsar and Fatherland." Her brother Friedrich Wilhelm served as her knight. Nicholas commissioned a Gothic Cottage at Alexandria Park in Peterhof in 1827 for Alexandra. The shield from the 1829 tournament, with Alexandra's personal emblem, was prominently featured in the decoration of the Cottage both inside and out, for example in the outside gables of the Palace as well as the chair backs of the dining room. The service for the Cottage Palace, which became known as the Cottage Palace Services, included both porcelain and glassware services. The shield was also featured in both the glass and porcelain services. (*photo page 38*)

107. **Cup and Saucer from the Cottage Service**, hard-paste porcelain, Imperial Porcelain Factory, Russia, cup 1900, saucer 1896, cup: 2 ¼ x 4 inches, saucer: 5 ¼ inches diameter. Each piece is marked under the base in green underglaze with the cipher of Nicholas II and dates. (*photo page 38*)

108. **Coffee pot from the Cottage Service**, hard-paste porcelain, Imperial Porcelain Factory, Russia, c. 1830, 8 x 6 ½ x 4 inches. The pot is marked under the base in underglaze blue with the cipher of Nicholas I. (*not pictured*)

109. **Custard Cup from the Cottage Service**, hard-paste porcelain, Imperial Porcelain Factory, Russia, c. 1900, 2 ½ x 3 ⅝ inches. The base is

106, 107 & 111

113

38 THE TSARS' CABINET

110. **Teapot from the Cottage Service**, hard-paste porcelain, Imperial Porcelain Factory, Russia, c. 1885, 5 ½ x 10 x 5 inches. (*not pictured*)

111 & 112. **Two Dessert Plates from the Gothic Cottage Dessert Service**, hard-paste porcelain, Imperial Porcelain Factory, Russia, c. 1885, 8 ⅝ inches diameter. In 1831, the service for the Cottage Palace was supplemented with a group of dessert plates designed to resemble Rose windows in Gothic cathedrals, consistent with the Gothic Revival design of the Cottage Palace. (*photos, page 38; detail page 20*)

113. **Teapot from the Gothic Service**, hard-paste porcelain, Imperial Porcelain Factory, Russia, c. 1833, 6 x 9 x 5 ½ inches. Echoing the Gothic design of the Cottage Palace was the service commissioned for the Winter Palace and presented to Nicholas I in 1833. The decoration was based on medieval motifs, such as stained glass windows. This service was repeatedly supplemented through the 19th and early 20th centuries and was often used during imperial parties and ceremonial banquets at the beginning of the 20th century. The handle of this teapot is formed as a neoclassical woman emerging from a leafy cornucopia and the lid finial has a helmeted female warrior. Both are entirely finished in matte gilding. The sides and lid are decorated in red, blue, green and black to resemble Gothic stained glass windows. (*photo page 38*)

114. **Dessert Plate from the Kremlin Service**, hard-paste porcelain, Imperial Porcelain Factory, Russia, c. 1840–1855, 8 ¾ inches diameter. The reverse of the plate has the blue underglaze mark for Nicholas I period and the red overglaze inventory number "21971." The design by Fedor Solntsev (1801–1892) is based on the jeweled, gold and enamel plate belonging to Tsar Alexei Mikhailovich. (*photo page 39*)

115. **Charger from the Kremlin Service**, hard-paste porcelain, Imperial Porcelain Factory, Russia, c. 1840–1855, 14 inches diameter. The charger is marked with the cipher of Nicholas I and also has a Kremlin inventory number in overglaze red. The design by Fedor Solntsev (1801–1892) is based on a Turkish washbasin made for Tsarina Natalya Naryshkina. (*photo page 19*)

116. **Compote from the Kremlin Service**, hard-paste porcelain, Imperial Porcelain Factory, Russia, c. 1855–1881, 4 x 8 ¾ x 9 inches. The design by Fedor Solntsev (1801–1892) is based on a Turkish washbasin made for Tsarina Natalya Naryshkina. (*not pictured*)

117. **Cup and Saucer from the Kremlin Service**, hard-paste porcelain, Imperial Porcelain Factory, Russia, saucer 1890, cup 1899, cup: 2 ¼ x 4 x 3 ¼ inches, saucer: 5 ¼ inches diameter. The design by Fedor Solntsev (1801–1892) is based on a Turkish washbasin made for Tsarina Natalya Naryshkina. (*photo page 19*)

118. **Bowl from the Kremlin Service**, hard-paste porcelain, Imperial Porcelain Factory, Russia, c. 1840–1855, 3 ¼ x 7 inches. The bowl is marked with the cipher of Nicholas I. The design by Fedor Solntsev (1801–1892) is based on a Turkish washbasin made for Tsarina Natalya Naryshkina. (*photo page 19*)

119. **Soup Plate from the Kremlin Service**, hard-paste porcelain, Imperial Porcelain Factory, Russia, c. 1840–1855, 9 inches diameter. The design by Fedor Solntsev (1801–1892) is based on a Turkish washbasin made for Tsarina Natalya Naryshkina. (*not pictured*)

120. **Soup Bowl from the Kremlin Service**, hard-paste porcelain, Imperial Porcelain Factory, Russia, c. 1840–1855, 2 x 9 ¾ inches. The bowl is marked with Nicholas I's cipher in underglaze blue, also with overglaze red Kremlin inventory number "OX.2167." (*not pictured*)

121. **Soup Tureen from the Service for Grand Duke Konstantin Nikolaevich**, hard-paste porcelain, Imperial Porcelain Factory, Russia, 1848–1852, 10 ¾ x 16 x 13 inches. The service was designed by Fedor Solntsev (1801–1892). The vessel lids for the service were topped with finials modeled after Tsar Alexei Mikhailovich's (1629–1676) gold helmet. (*photos page 40, detail page 20*)

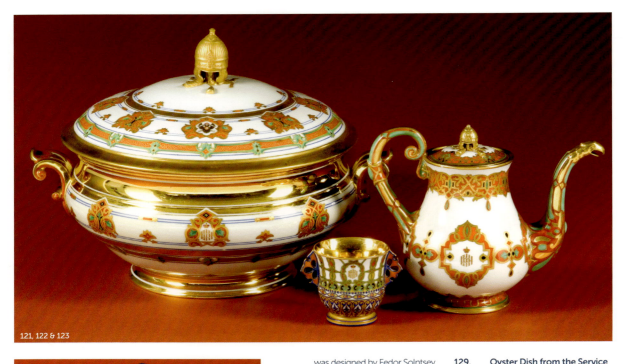

121, 122 & 123

129

122. **Custard Cup from the Service for Grand Duke Konstantin Nikolaevich**, hard-paste porcelain, Imperial Porcelain Factory, Russia, 1848–1852, 3 x 4 x 3 inches. The custard cup is marked under the base with an underglaze "N I" for Nicholas I. The Service was designed by Fedor Solntsev (1801–1892). (*photo page 40*)

123. **Teapot from the Service for Grand Duke Konstantin Nikolaevich**, hard-paste porcelain, Imperial Porcelain Factory, Russia, 1848–1852, 7 ½ x 9 x 5 inches. The Service was designed by Fedor Solntsev (1801–1892). (*photo page 40*)

124. **Plate from the Service for Grand Duke Konstantin Nikolaevich**, hard-paste porcelain, Imperial Porcelain Factory, Russia, 1848–1852, 9 ½ inches diameter. The Service was designed by Fedor Solntsev (1801–1892). (*not pictured*)

125. **Cordial from the Service for Grand Duke Konstantin Nikolaevich**, glass, Imperial Glassworks, Russia, 1848–1852, 4 ½ x 2 inches. (*not pictured*)

126. **Sauce Boat and Stand from the Service for Grand Duke Konstantin Nikolaevich**, hard-paste porcelain, Imperial Porcelain Factory, Russia, 1848–1852, 6 x 10 x 7 inches. The service was designed by Fedor Solntsev (1801–1892). (*not pictured*)

127. **Dessert Plate from the Service for Grand Duke Konstantin Nikolaevich**, hard-paste porcelain, Imperial Porcelain Factory, Russia, 1848–1852, 8 ¾ inches diameter. The service was designed by Fedor Solntsev (1801–1892). (*not pictured*)

128. **Charka from the Service for Grand Duke Konstantin Nikolaevich**, hard-paste porcelain, Imperial Porcelain Factory, Russia, 1848–1852, 2 x 3 ½ x 2 ½ inches. The service was designed by Fedor Solntsev (1801–1892). (*not pictured*)

129. **Oyster Dish from the Service for Grand Duke Konstantin Nikolaevich**, hard-paste porcelain, Imperial Porcelain Factory, Russia, 1848–1852, 5 inches diameter. The service was designed by Fedor Solntsev (1801–1892). Raised on a circular rim, the concave dish has a scalloped rim and trefoil handle displaying the Imperial Eagle against a gilt ground and within a strapwork reserve. The borders and interior are similarly decorated. The underside is marked with blue underglaze cipher of Nicholas I under the Imperial crown. (*photo page 40*)

130 & 131. **Campana Urns Illustrating the Arts**, hard-paste porcelain, Imperial Porcelain Factory, Russia, c. 1845, 27 x 19 x 19 inches. The central bodies of this pair of urns are painted with neoclassical designs and each have circular cartouches containing various classical figures studying the arts. Urn 130 features "Writing" on one side and "Painting" on the other. Urn 131 features "Architecture" on one side and "Sculpture" on the other. The cartouches are encircled with gilded and tooled bands against black grounds and each is separated by a cornucopia and gilt scrolls and shells. The central bodies of the urns are bordered top and bottom with belts of white and gilt arches. The lower

130 (side featuring Writing)

130 (side featuring Painting)

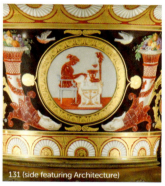
131 (side featuring Architecture)

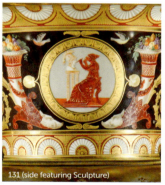
131 (side featuring Sculpture)

130 & 131 (handle detail)

130 & 131 (side detail)

bodies are molded and gilded with raised acanthus leaves, rosettes and rocaille and further mounted with handles having rams head attachments. The upper rims and bases are heavily gilded. Each urn rests upon a gilded bronze square-form base.

The urns were possibly made for the pavilion of Tsaritsin, which was designed for the Empress Alexandra Feodorovna by Andrei Stackenschneider (1802–1865) in 1839 and sited on an island in the lake of Olga, named after the Empress' daughter Grand Duchess Olga. (*photo page 41*)

132. **Plate from the Etruscan Service**, hard-paste porcelain, Imperial Porcelain Factory, Russia, c. 1845, 8 ¾ inches diameter. The cavetto is decorated with a classical figure of a woman standing holding a trident in one hand and a halo of leaves in the other. She is bordered by a spray of foliage on the left and an urn resting upon a pedestal on the right. The border is finished with a band of classical arabesques. As with the majority of this service, this plate's detail is in black against an orange ground with a few dark red highlights. (*photo page 42*)

133. **Plate in the Etruscan Style**, hard-paste porcelain, Imperial Porcelain Factory, Russia, c. 1845, 9 ½ inches diameter. The cavetto on this plate is painted in red and black with a classical scene of a standing female figure holding a bucket in her right hand and an oval object in her left hand with a three-legged table in front of her. The edge of the cavetto and the border of the plate are painted with bands of neo-classical decoration in black. This decoration is painted against an unusual beige ground, as opposed to the more typical brick red grounds generally seen in the Etruscan Service. (*photo page 42*)

134. **Teapot in the Etruscan Style**, hard-paste porcelain, Imperial Porcelain Factory, Russia, c. 1845, 4 ¾ x 7 x 4 inches. This teapot has a bulbous body and narrowed neck. The inverted rim, curved spout and loop handle are painted black. The body and the neck are black and orange with swans, palmettes and scroll ornament. There is a flat lid with a pointed knop finial. (*photo page 42*)

135. **Compote in the Etruscan Style**, hard-paste porcelain,

42 THE TSARS' CABINET

Imperial Porcelain Factory, Russia, c. 1845, 2 ½ x 8 ¾ x 8 ¾ inches. The center of this bowl is painted with a classical-style seated woman holding a box in one hand and a bucket in the other, against a white ground. The border and exterior of the compote are finished in dark orange with black highlights. (*photo page 42*)

136. **Plate in the Etruscan Style**, hard-paste porcelain, Imperial Porcelain Factory, Russia, c. 1845, 8 ½ inches diameter. The cavetto is painted with a man on a chariot in red and black on a white ground. The border is finished in dark orange with black highlights. (*photo page 42*)

137. **Palace Urn**, hard-paste porcelain, Imperial Porcelain Factory, Russia, c. 1845, 27 x 13 ½ x 10 inches. The urn has a tall, cylindrical form with a high shoulder, flaring rim and spreading foot. It is mounted right and left with large, high handles finished with both matte and bright gilding. The front of the urn has a rectangular cartouche finely painted with the portrait of an 18th century gentleman. The lower portion of the body is wrapped with raised classical style leaves painted yellow against a gilded ground, the balance of the body finished in powder blue with gilded highlights. (*photo page 43*)

138. **Plate from the Mikhailovskii Service**, hard-paste porcelain, Imperial Porcelain Factory, Russia, c. 1840, 10 ¼ inches diameter. The cavetto is finely painted with a European scene, and the border finished with green and gilded arabesques. It is marked under the base with the Nicholas I cipher in underglaze blue. The Mikhailovskii Service was made for the palace of that name, built for Grand Duke Michael Pavlovich, Emperor Alexander I's and Emperor Nicholas I's youngest brother. (*photo page 43*)

139. **Tureen from the Grand Duchess Ekaterina Mikhailovna Service**, hard-paste porcelain, Imperial Porcelain Factory, Russia, c. 1840, 12 x 17 x 12 inches. Grand Duchess Ekaterina Mikhailovna was the daughter of Grand Duke Michael Pavlovich, and married Duke Georg August of Mecklenburg-Strelitz. (*photo page 43*)

140. **Egg**, hard-paste porcelain, Imperial Porcelain Factory, Russia, c. 1830–1855, 3 ½ inches, 4 ⅞ inches

141 (front)

141 (back)

with stand. Marked near the lower opening with the rare impressed Nicholas I mark. The egg is mounted on its original gilt metal stand. The egg has oval cartouches with religious symbols, a dove on one side and a chalice on the other, both over clouds, in tooled gilding. (not pictured)

141. **Egg**, hard-paste porcelain, Imperial Porcelain Factory, Russia, c. 1890, 8 ½ inches length, with ribbon. Easter was the most important Christian festival for the Russian church. The practice of celebrating the Resurrection of Christ by exchanging Easter eggs came to Russia from Byzantium. According to Byzantine historian Nikoforos Callistius, Mary Magdalene appeared before the Roman Emperor Tiberius and presented him with a red egg, which symbolized Christ's sacrifice and His Resurrection. Eggs of all materials were presented by tsars to courtiers and other distinguished people, along with other gifts, on Easter and the following days. Alexander III later ordered that only eggs would be used as Easter presents. Eggs could be decorated with scenes of saints. This egg is painted with a miniature of St. Aleksei, Metropolitan of Moscow, after a design by Osip S. Chirikov. The reverse has a cross, centered with an image of Christ Pantocrator, with each point finished with saints and angels, designed by A.S. Kaminskii. (photo page 44)

142. **Egg**, hard-paste porcelain, Imperial Porcelain Factory, Russia, c 1830–1850, length 5 inches. The egg is painted with a scene of St. Joseph. (not pictured)

143 & 144. **Plaques**, hard-paste porcelain, Imperial Porcelain Factory, Russia, c. 1841, 10 ⅞ x 9 ¼ x ¼ inches and 10 ⅜ x 8 ⅝ x ¼ inches. The first plaque depicts a kneeling monk reading a book, signed in the lower right by Semionov, and is marked on the reverse with a painted inventory number "53" and applied inventory labels "O.N. no 135" and "227 O.N." The second plaque depicts a monk praying with his hands clasped on top of a book in front of a crucifix, is signed in the lower right "C.R.B. du Moor" and dated 1841. The reverse is marked with an underglaze "N" in blue and the painted inventory number "52." (photo page 45)

145. **Egg**, hard-paste porcelain, Imperial Porcelain Factory, Russia, second half of the 19th century, 4 inches length. The egg is decorated with a stylized garland with crosses. (not pictured)

146. **Tureen and Stand**, hard-paste porcelain, Imperial Porcelain Factory, Russia, c. 1860, 12 ½ x 14 ½ x 12 on stand. This tureen and stand is from a service designed after a Sèvres service given by Louis XV to Christian VII of Denmark in 1768. The entire body, lid and stand are all decorated with oblong cartouches filled with brightly colored, floral sprays against white grounds. The rest of the grounds are covered with gilded, egg-shaped ovals against cobalt. The finial, handles and borders are finished with heavy, bright gilding. (photo page 45)

147. **Decanter and six Cordials from the Banqueting Service**, glass, Imperial Glassworks, Russia, c. 1840–1855, decanter: 13 inches height, cordials: 4 ½ inches height. In 1824, the Imperial Glass Factory developed a design that was used for Imperial family members throughout the 19th century. Encased in the glass was a thin sheet of gold, painted to resemble the Imperial ermine and monogrammed with the individual's initials. The general type came to be called Banqueting Services. This is the decanter set made for Emperor Alexander II while he was tsarevich, a Slavic title given to the tsar's heir, with his enameled cipher. (photo page 45)

148. **Cup and Saucer**, hard-paste porcelain, Imperial Porcelain Factory, Russia, cup: 3rd quarter of the 19th century, 2 ¾ x 4 ¼ x 3 ¼ inches, saucer: 1883, saucer: 5 ⅝ inches diameter. The cup is marked with the cipher of Emperor Alexander II and the saucer is marked with the cipher of Emperor Alexander III and dated 1883. This

146

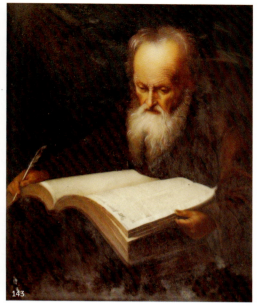

143

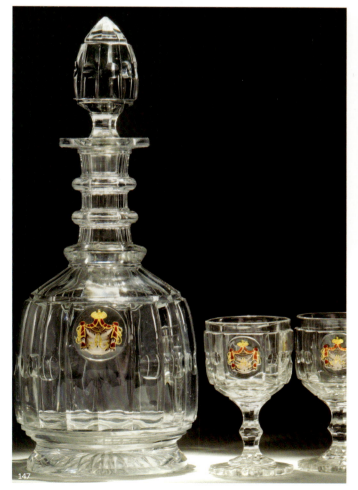

147

144

service was made for Emperor Alexander III while he was tsarevich. The cup is painted with a crowned Imperial Eagle, wings spread and with a gilded "A" on its breast, and is covered with floral sprays. (*not pictured*)

149. **Plate from the Service for the Yacht Derzhava**, hard-paste porcelain, Imperial Porcelain Factory, Russia, c. 1871, 9 ¾ inches diameter. The plate is marked with an underglaze green mark of Alexander II. The yacht services were perhaps the most private of all those made in the 19th century, as they were intended for the Imperial family and their

45

150, 151 & 152

companions. The items are practically shaped, heavier and squatter, for greater stability on shipboard, than similar wares for the palaces. One of the yachts was named Derzhava, which is the Russian word for "orb," and in this instance refers to the orb held in the talons of the double-headed eagle in the state seal. Pieces in this service are decorated with nautical motifs of chains, ropes and anchors. The chains and ropes are interwoven in a manner reminiscent of Old Russian strapwork in the form of the double headed eagle. The orb and Alexander II's cipher in Old Slavonic are shown on the border of the plate. This service was designed by Ippolit Monigetti (1819–1878). (*not pictured*)

150. **Cup and Saucer from the Service for the Yacht Livadia**, hard-paste porcelain, Imperial Porcelain Factory, Russia, c. 1885, cup: 3 x 4 ½ x 3 ¼ inches, saucer: 6 ½ inches diameter. The yacht Livadia was named after the Livadia Palace in the Crimea. This service was produced in 1871–1873, and ornamented in the style of the French King Louis XVI, which matched the interior of the yacht. The ornamentation includes laurel branches, and ship chains, along with medallions with crowns and the monograms of Emperor Alexander II and his wife Maria. (*photo page 46*)

151. **Plate from the Service for the Yacht Derzhava**, hard-paste porcelain, Imperial Porcelain Factory, Russia, c. 1855–1881, 9 ⅛ inches diameter. This plate is a later design for the Derzhava, which has the orb with the St. Andrew ensign and navy jack, or flag. (*photo page 46*)

152. **Bowl from the Yacht Derzhava**, hard-paste porcelain, Imperial Porcelain Factory, Russia, 1889, 3 ½ x 7 x 7 ¼ inches. The bowl is marked under its base with Alexander III's cipher in underglaze green and dated 1889. This bowl for a later service for the Derzhava. (*photo, page 46*)

153. **Sherbet Cup from the Yacht Polar Star**, glass, Imperial Glassworks, Russia, c. 1888, 5 x 3 ½ inches. Tsar Alexander III commissioned the Polar Star yacht in 1888 and it was launched two years later. The Dowager Empress used it for her annual trips to Denmark. No porcelain was designed for this yacht, but glassware for this yacht was engraved with the Imperial Eagle. (*not pictured*)

154. **Vodka Cup from the Yacht Shtandart**, glass, Imperial Glassworks, Russia, c. 1895, 3 ½ x 1 ¾ inches. The Shtandart, was the favored yacht of Nicholas II and Alexandra and was built during his reign. Shtandart was named for the Russian Imperial Standard, the flag used by the emperor. (*not pictured*)

155. **Decanter from the Yacht Onega**, glass, Imperial Glassworks, Russia, c. 1855–1881, 6 x 2 ¾ inches. (*not pictured*)

156. **The Durnovo Casket**, silver gilt, enamel and sheets of lapis lazuli, Firm of Ovchinnikov, Russia, 1889, 6 ½ x 13 ½ x 9 ¼ inches. Pavel Ovchinnikov was a former serf of Prince Sergei Volkonsky and a graduate of the Strogonov School. The Strogonov School was founded in Moscow in 1860 to encourage artists to work in a Russian Style that incorporated ancient Russian church and folk designs. Ovchinnikov opened his silver and enamelwork factory in Moscow in 1853, and was working in the Old Russian Style by the late 1860s. He was awarded the Imperial warrant in 1868. Imperial warrants were issued to those who provided goods to the Imperial court. In addition to wining numerous medals at All Russian exhibitions, the factory won a Gold medal in Paris in 1889. After his death in 1888, his sons continued to run the factory.

This casket was made by the Ovchinnikov firm in 1889, and

was presented to Ivan Nikolaevich Durnovo in 1889, as indicated by the coat of arms and inscription on the top. In 1886, after holding a number of other offices, Durnovo was appointed Director of the Fourth Department of His Imperial Majesty's Office that was in charge of Charitable Institutions of Empress Maria and Chairman of its Council of Trustees. He served in that position until May 6, 1889, when he was appointed Minister of the Interior under Alexander III. In 1895, he became Chairman of the Tsar's Council of Ministers under Nicholas II, until his death in 1903.

The Charitable Institutions of Empress Maria was founded in 1796. By 1889, it was entrusted with 500 charities. The official emblem of the foundation was the pelican feeding three young birds in the nest, which is shown on a plaque on the side of the casket. The casket was most likely presented by all the members of the council to Mr. Durnovo as a going away present. Traditionally, the box would contain the photographs of the various institutions that were part of the foundation.

The casket was offered for sale by the New York firm of Schaffer Galleries (A La Vielle Russie), as illustrated in the New York Sun in 1938. During the 1920s and 1930s, the Soviet government sold many pieces through various American retailers, such as Schaffer and Armand Hammer, in an effort to raise funds. The casket was later given to His Excellency H. K'ung, Minister of Finance of China during World War II, 75th lineal descendent of Confucius and the brother-in-law of Chiang Kai-shek. (*photo page 47*)

156

156 (top)

157. **Plate from the Raphael Service**, hard-paste porcelain, Imperial Porcelain Factory, Russia, 1903, 9 ½ inches diameter. The center of this plate is finely painted en grisaille with a semi-clad, seated woman in classical style against a red ground hexagonal panel. The rim has three seated classical figures, each reading, writing or teaching from stone tablets, each within circular panels of red grounds. The three figures are separated by panels and borders of classical motifs in various shades of gray. (*photos pages 21 & 48*)

158. **Plate from the Raphael Service**, hard-paste porcelain, Imperial Porcelain Factory, Russia, 1884, 7 inches diameter. The center of this side plate is finely painted *en grisaille* with a semi-clad, seated female figure reaching out to a putto, in classical style, against a green ground hexagonal panel. The rim has three putti, each within circular panels of green grounds. The three figures are separated by finely and brightly painted panels of classical peoples and landscapes, further highlighted with borders of classical motifs. (*photo, pages 21 & 48*)

159. **Soup plate from the Raphael Service**, hard-paste porcelain, Imperial Porcelain Factory, Russia, 1884, 9 ⅝ inches diameter. The center of this plate is finely painted *en grisaille* with a winged putto holding an arrow. He is leaning in and touching the arm of a semi-clad, seated woman viewed against a grey ground hexagonal panel. The rim has three circular cartouches, each containing classical figures (part man and part beasts) against red grounds. The three cartouches are separated by panels and borders of classical motifs in various shades of gray. (*photos pages 21 & 48*)

160. **Dessert Plate from the Raphael Service**, hard-paste porcelain, Imperial Porcelain Factory, Russia, 1884, 8 ⅜ inches diameter. The cavetto of this plate is painted with a scene of a man, woman and child in classical dress. The rim has three cartouches with cherubs. (*photos pages 21 & 48*)

157

158

159

160

161

162

48 THE TSARS' CABINET

161. **Cup and Saucer from the Raphael Service**, hard-paste porcelain, Imperial Porcelain Factory, Russia, 1894, cup: 2 ¼ x 3 ¼ x 3 inches, saucer: 4 5/8 inches diameter. The cup is finely painted *en grisaille* in classical style, with a putto riding a dragon, a tree in front and a bush behind them, against red panels. The cup also has secondary paneled scenes, all separated by beautiful classical arabesques. The saucer is fully painted with connecting arabesques *en suite*. (*photos pages 21 & 48*)

162. **Butter plate from the Raphael Service**, hard-paste porcelain, Imperial Porcelain Factory, Russia, 1889, 5 ¾ inches diameter. This plate is painted with a classical scene against a red ground bordered with foliage scrolls and stylized creatures. (*photos pages 21 & 48*)

163. **Khodynka Field Coronation Cup**, enamel, Russia, 1896, 4 x 3 x 3 ¾ inches. The Russian people could collect one of these souvenir cups with beer at a large celebration held on the Khodynkovo Meadow in Moscow on the occasion of the Coronation of Nicholas II.

It was customary to provide a feast and gifts for the people. People had traveled from all over Russia to celebrate and to get a glimpse of the new Emperor and Empress. At least half a million people were at Khodynkovo Meadow, a field used for military drills outside of Moscow, where wooden tables were set up over ditches. There was a stampede, the cause of which was not determined, and at least 1,300 people were trampled to death. While the Emperor and Empress made an appearance at the field that day, the scene was hidden from them by tarpaulins and a hasty clean up. Later that night, they attended a ball given in their honor by the French ambassador. While Nicholas and Alexandra were reportedly distraught by the events, the effect of the disaster and their subsequent activities made a negative impression on the Russian people. This coronation cup was owned by Vladimir Horowitz. (*not pictured*)

164. **Dessert Plate from the Service for the Tsarevich Nikolai Aleksandrovich (the future Nicholas II)**, hard-paste porcelain, Imperial Porcelain Factory, Russia, 1888, 8 ½ inches diameter. Dated 1888 with the mark of Tsar Alexander III. (*photo page 49*)

165. **Wineglass from the Nikolai Aleksandrovich Service**, glass, Imperial Glass Factory, Russia, c. 1913, 6 ¼ x 2 ½ inches. The glass is engraved by Lavr Orlovskii, recalling the designs of the mid-18th century under Empresses Elizabeth and Catherine.

Several of the important cultural events of Nicholas II's reign incorporated earlier styles. The Imperial Ball of 1903, the last one held at the Winter Palace, featured 17th century court dress. Nicholas was dressed in the style of Tsar Alexei, while Alexandra wore the attire of his first wife, Maria Miloslavskaia. In 1913, the Tercentenary of the founding of the Romanov dynasty provided another opportunity for Nicholas to associate himself with 17th century Russia.

166. **Imperial Presentation Portfolio**, leather, silver, enamel, gems, Firm of Fabergé, Russia, c. 1900, 15 ¼ x 11 ½ x 1 inches. The portfolio has the cipher of Nicholas II, and was owned by John Williams of Savannah (made famous in the book *Midnight of the Garden of Good and Evil*). (*not pictured*)

167. **Egg**, porcelain, Imperial Porcelain Factory, Russia, 1910–1916, 7 inches length with ribbon. The egg has the cipher of Alexandra Fedorovna and garlands in green and teal on a white ground. One category of decoration of eggs was the cipher, or monogram, of the tsar or member of the royal family presenting the egg, a category that was established during the reign of Alexander III. These eggs were on a red or white ground, with frames of ornamental designs and garlands. (*not pictured*)

168. **Plate from the Purple Service for the Tsarskosel'skii Palace**, hard-paste porcelain, Imperial Porcelain Factory, Russia, 1905, 9 ¾ inches diameter. The border of this plate is decorated with alternating cartouches, four with tooled matte gilding separated by four beautifully painted forest scenes in shades of purple, the color of sovereignty. The cavetto is painted with a cherub. This was the last major commission produced by the Imperial Porcelain Factory for the court. (*photo page 49*)

169. **Vase**, hard-paste porcelain, Imperial Porcelain Factory,

Russia, c. 1900, 8 x 5 ½ inches. In the Old Russian Style, the body is wrapped with strapwork and three semicircular cartouches, which have stylized leaves. The Old Russian style of pre-Petrine motifs was refined further in the late 19th century. From the arts and crafts movements of Europe, Moscow's artists combined the art nouveau motifs with the Old Russian Style folk motifs to create a style moderne. (*not pictured*)

170. **Beaker**, hard-paste porcelain, Kuznetsov Factory, Russia, 1899, 3 ¾ x 2 ½ x 2 ½ inches. The red beaker covered with strapwork of gilding and blue has a shaped cartouche containing the Cyrillic monogram "P.A." above the dates "1874–1899." (*not pictured*)

171. **Cigar Case**, gilded silver and shaded cloisonné enamel, Fedor Rückert for Firm of Fabergé, Russia, 1908–1916, 6 ½ x 9 ½ inches in the original holly wood case. One who excelled in the Old Russian style was Fedor Ruckert. An independent workmaster, Ruckert supplied Faberge's Moscow store with enamels. He excelled in the use of shaded enamels and unusual color combinations. He also used wires to create their own patterns and not just to separate color. The interior of this cigar case is engraved in Russian, "Dear Sasha from the person who loves him very much, Leekee 1916." (*photo page 50*)

172. **Kovsh**, silver-mounted ceramic with cabochon colored stones, Firm of Fabergé, Russia, 1908–1917, 3 ¾ x 7 ¼ x 5 inches. (*not pictured*)

173. **Cigarette Case**, gunmetal, gold, diamonds, sapphire, by an unidentified workmaster, attributed possibly to Viktor Fink or V. Finikov, Russia, before 1896, 2 x 5 x 7 inches. Case has incised lines, with diamonds in the intersections. (*photo page 50*)

174. **Cigarette Case**, Palisander wood, two-colored gold, diamonds and pearls, Fabergé, Russia, c. 1900, 3 ¼ x 4 ¼ inches in original holly wood box. (*photo page 50*)

175. **Lukutin Lacquer Box**, lacquer, with gilded-silver mounts, Firm of Fabergé, workmaster Anders Nevalainen, St. Petersburg, Russia, 1896–1908, 1 ½ x 2 ⅛ inches. The box has the Fabergé scratched inventory "# 9226." (*photo page 50*)

176. **Chamberstick**, ceramic, silver mounts, Firm of Fabergé, Moscow, Russia, 1896–1908, 2 ½ x 7 x 4 ½ inches. (*photo page 50*)

177. **Scent Bottle**, ceramic, silver mounts, Cabochon Sapphire finial, Firm of Fabergé, workmaster Andrei Gorianov, St. Petersburg, Russia, 1908–1917, height 3 ¼ inches. The bottle is in Chinese style with a crackle glaze. The top mount has two concentric bands of decoration: a reed and tie design, and a Greek key design. The foot has a band of acanthus leaves. The cork mounted reeded stopper has a cabochon sapphire finial. (*not pictured*)

178. **Court Photograph**, photograph, Russia, 1892, 8 x 5 inches. An original court photograph of Grand Duke Sergei and Grand Duchess Elizabeth in mourning attire, possibly related to the death of her father, Grand Duke Louis of Hesse, signed "Uncle Serge and Aunt Ella," dated 1892.

One of the most intriguing persons in Russia at this time was Grand Duchess Elizabeth. She spent her early years in glittering court life, but turned away from that existence to attempt to make a difference in the lives of everyday people. In the process, she was martyred and is now recognized as a saint. Along with nine others, she is honored as a representative of the 20th century martyrs of Christendom on the West Front of Westminster Abbey in London.

Grand Duchess Elizabeth was born Elizabeth (Ella), Princess of Hesse in 1864, a granddaughter of Queen Victoria. Her mother named her after an ancestor of the Hessian dynasty, St. Elizabeth of Hungary, who, after her husband died in the crusades, became a nun, gave away her possessions, founded hospitals and devoted herself to the poor.

She was the older sister of Alix (christened Victoria Alix Helena Louise Beatrice), who married Nicholas II and became Alexandra Fedorovna. Another sister, Victoria, married Louis Prince of Battenberg and was Phillip Duke of Edinburgh's grandmother. After Ella's mother died of diphtheria in 1878, she and her sisters spent part of the remainder of their childhood with their grandmother in England.

Grand Duchess Elizabeth was regarded as one of the most beautiful princesses in Europe. In 1884, she married one of Emperor Alexander III's younger brothers, Grand Duke Sergei Aleksandrovich. This proved to be a difficult marriage. While she led an elegant life, she also channeled her religious devotion to the Orthodox religion, to which she converted in 1891. She was instrumental in her sister's marriage to Nicholas II in 1894.

Grand Duke Sergei was the Governor of Moscow and was assassinated in the Kremlin in 1905. Following his murder, Elizabeth turned more to religion. She founded a sisterhood of nuns dedicated to nursing and charity, which was unique in the Orthodox church, in which nuns typically did not venture into the outside world. She established various charitable institutions, including a hospital, orphanage, hospice, etc. She tried to warn her sister against Rasputin, who she considered a fraud.

After the Revolution, she was imprisoned in the Urals, and murdered along with five Romanovs and one of her nuns at Alapayevsk on July 17, 1918, the day after her sister, Empress Alexandra, Emperor Nicholas and their children were murdered at Yekaterinburg. Her remains and those of her fellow victims were recovered by Father Seraphim, her confessor, who transported the coffins through Siberia and China to Beijing. Her sister Victoria arranged to have her remains transported to Jerusalem, where she was buried at a church at the foot of Mount of Olives. She was canonized as a martyr to communist persecution by the church abroad in 1984 and by the Moscow Patriarchate in 1992. (*not pictured*)

179. **Postcard Photograph**, Russia, 1914, 5 ½ x 3 ½ inches. An original photo postcard of Grand Duchess Ella after she entered the convent, signed at the base "Elizabeth 1914". (*photo page 52*)

180. **Egg**, hard-paste porcelain, Imperial Porcelain Factory, Russia, c. 1900, 6 ½ inches length, with ribbon. The egg is adorned with the gilded, crowned Cyrillic name of Grand Duke Sergei with the letters interlocked and running vertically down the body of the egg. On the reverse is the coat of arms of the city of Moscow.

Eggs received as gifts were hung around icons in special cases. The ribbons added to the

(top row) 179, (middle row) 180, 182, 181, (bottom row) 183 & 184

eggs were silk, *moiré*, or velvet and came in various colors, textures and patterns. The ribbon had a loop at the top for hanging and, at the bottom, it was tied with a bow or has a rosette. (*photo page 52*)

181. **Egg**, hard-paste porcelain, Imperial Porcelain Factory, Russia, c. 1900, 6 ½ inches length, with ribbon. The egg has the crowned Cyrillic name of Grand Duchess Elizabeth, running horizontally across the egg. Each white-bodied egg is mounted with a silk tassel. (*photo page 52*)

182. **Egg**, hard-paste porcelain, Imperial Porcelain Factory, Russia, c. 1900, 3 inches length. The egg has a block letter "E" in green, for Grand Duchess Elizabeth, surrounded by a raised and tooled gilded wreath and surmounted by a gilded Imperial crown. There is a wreath tied with four green ties. (*photo page 52*)

183. **Egg**, hard-paste porcelain, Imperial Porcelain Factory, Russia, c. 1900, 4 ½ inches length, with ribbon. The egg is painted with the Cyrillic initials "ES" for Grand Duke Sergei and Grand Duchess Elizabeth, within a gilt ribbon-tied laurel wreath surmounted by an Imperial crown. (*photo page 52*)

184. **Egg**, hard-paste porcelain, Imperial Porcelain Factory, Russia, c. 1900, 3 inches length. The egg has the crowned Imperial cipher of Grand Duke Sergei Aleksandrovich in red against a white ground. (*photo page 52*)

185. **Knife, Fork and Spoon**, gilded silver, Firm of Fabergé, Russia, 1884–1894, knife: 10 ½ inches, fork: 7 ¼ inches, spoon: 7 ¼ inches. Each piece is in the Firm of Fabergé neoclassical swan pattern. The handle of each piece incorporates an oval-shaped cartouche formed by a wreath of leaves, engraved with the Imperial cipher of Grand Duchess Elizabeth. (*not pictured*)

186 & 187. **Postcard and Postcard Letter**, Russia, 1908–1911, 3 ½ x 5 ½ inches. The correspondence is from Grand Duchess Elizabeth to Miss Nona Kerr, the lady in waiting of her sister, Princess Victoria of Battenberg. (*not pictured*)

188. **Bowl**, faience, Russia, 1910–1917, 3 x 4 ¾ inches. The bowl is for one of the hospital charities that Grand Duchess Elizabeth supported. The white body has a bright-blue text describing the charity and a crowned shield-shaped cartouche bearing her Imperial cipher. (*not pictured*)

189. **Egg**, hard-paste porcelain, Imperial Porcelain Factory, Russia, 1890–1900s, 3 ½ inches length. The egg has the cipher of Maria Fedorovna. Red was an important color for an egg, as it symbolized the blood of Christ, His death and Resurrection. (*photo page 53*)

190. **Cup and Saucer**, hard-paste porcelain, Royal Copenhagen, Denmark, c. 1870–1890, cup: 2 ¼ x 5 x 4 ¼ inches, saucer: 6 ¼ inches diameter. The cup has the monogram of Alexander III. (*not pictured*)

191. **Vase**, hard-paste porcelain, Imperial Porcelain Factory, Russia, c. 1900–1910, 9 ⅝ x 3 ⅝ x 5 ¼ inches. Scene painted in the art nouveau style of the Royal Copenhagen Factory. (*photo page 53*)

192. **Vase**, glass, Imperial Glass Factory, Russia, 1912, 14 ¼ x 8 x 8 inches. The vase is carved with flowers and foliage in an art nouveau style with brown cut clear, with a frosted finish. The vase was owned by Dowager Empress Maria Fedorovna, who kept it on her desk in Denmark, and then owned by Grand Duchess Olga Aleksandrovna.

Maria Fedorovna, the wife of Alexander III and mother of Nicholas II, was born Princess Dagmar of Denmark, the daughter of King Christian IX of Denmark and the sister of Queen Alexandra of England. After the fall of the Romanovs, she escaped through the Crimea and eventually settled at Hvidore, the house outside Copenhagen that she and her sister had purchased before the war. She was accompanied by her two daughters, Grand Duchesses Xenia and Olga. After her mother died in 1928, Olga settled on a farm in Denmark. In 1948, she emigrated to Canada, where she died in Toronto in 1960. (*photo page 54*)

193. **Bell**, silver, Russia, 1866, 1 ¾ x 2 ½ inches. The bell is engraved with the Imperial cipher of the Dowager Empress Maria Fedorovna. (It purportedly was the personal bell of the Empress and is from the estate of her daughter, Grand Duchess Olga.) (*not pictured*)

194. **Teaglass Holder**, copper, Firm of Fabergé, Russia, 1915, 3 ½ x 4 ½ x 3 inches.

189

191

53

The holder has medallions of the Imperial Eagle on one side and, on the other side, the Russian words for "War", 1914–1915 and "Fabergé."

Following the assassination of Grand Duke Franz Ferdinand and Grand Duchess Sophie in 1914, and the Austrian ultimatum against Serbia, Russia declared war on Austria. Initially, the country entered the war under a mood of national unity and patriotism. Crowds cheered the Tsar and his family in St. Petersburg. Propaganda and voluntary activity echoed this patriotism. Decorative arts made during the early years of the war reflected this attitude of patriotism and austerity. (*photo, page 54*)

195. **Egg**, hard-paste porcelain, Imperial Porcelain Factory, Russia, 1915, 2 ⅝ inches length. The egg has a gilded cipher of Emperor Nicholas II on one side and the gilded date 1915 on the other. (*not pictured*)

196. **Egg**, porcelain, Imperial Porcelain Factory, Russia, 1916, 3 ¾ inches length. The egg has the crowned gilded cipher of Empress Maria Fedorovna set in a cartouche surrounded by a gilded trellis. On the reverse is the date "1916" and a red cross. Eggs made during the years during World War I were particularly somber. During World War I, the Imperial Porcelain Factory made Easter eggs with red crosses for presentation to wounded soldiers in hospitals receiving the traditional Easter blessing. (*not pictured*)

197. **Cigarette Case**, two-colored gold, Firm of Fabergé, Russia, c. 1900, 3 ½ x 3 inches. The case has the cipher of Nikolas Nikolaevich. At the beginning of the war, the supreme commander of the Russian forces was Grand Duke Nicholas Nicholaevich, the grandson of Nicholas 1, and the cousin of Tsar Alexander III. Tall and imposing (he was referred to as a "bogatyr", or early Russian folk warrior), he was a professional soldier and well respected by his troops, but not a military strategist. He substantially disapproved of Rasputin and his increasing influence over Empress Alexandra. He was removed from command in 1915, generally at the insistence of Empress Alexandra, and reassigned to the Caucasian front. (*not pictured*)

198. **Compote**, bisque and hard-paste porcelain, Imperial Porcelain Factory, Russia, 1917, 6 x 9 ⅞ inches. This compote of bisque and glazed white porcelain is of classical form with foliate decoration in high relief molding on the exterior and foot. The interior is left elegantly plain with only a beaded top rim. This item is of two-piece construction with a bolt holding the foot to the body as seen in early 19th century production. Note that the Provisional mark was only used from April to December in 1917. In 1917, Emperor Nicholas II abdicated, and the Provisional government was formed, ending the reign of the Romanovs. (*photo page 54*)

199. **Plate**, hard-paste porcelain, Meissen Porcelain Factory, Germany, c. 1950, 10 inches diameter. The cavetto of this plate is painted in blue with a stylized scene of revolutionary soldiers storming the Winter Palace in 1917. (*photo page 55*)

BIBLIOGRAPHY
to *Russian Porcelain: Symbols Of Power and Identity* by Anne Odom (p. 11–21)

1. This article is based on previous research, much of it published in Anne Odom, *Russian Imperial Porcelain at Hillwood* (Washington, D.C.: Hillwood Museum & Gardens, 1999), and Anne Odom "The Politics of Porcelain," in *At the Tsar's Table: Russian Imperial Porcelain from the Raymond F. Piper Collection* (Milwaukee, Wisconsin: Marquette University, 2001, 11–22).

2. For dining customs throughout Europe, see Philippa Glanville and Hillary Young, *Elegant Eating: Four Hundred Years of Dining in Style* (London: V&A Publications, 2002).

3. Thomas DaCosta Kaufman, *Court, Cloister and City: The Art and Culture of Central Europe: The Art and Culture of Central Europe 1450–1800* (Chicago: University of Chicago Press, 1995), 308.

4. See Nataliia Sipovskaia, *farfor v Rossii XVIII veka* (Moscow: Pinakoteke, 2008),

5. Letter to Mrs. Robert Wilmot in *The Russian Journals of Martha and Catherine Wilmot*, eds. Edith Helen Vane-Tempest-Stewart and Montgomery H. Hyde (London: Macmillan and Co., Ltd., 1934), 81.

6. Henry Storch, *The Picture of St. Petersburg* (London: T.A. Longman, 1801), 555 and George E. Munro, "Food in Catherinian St. Petersburg," in *Food in Russian History and Culture*, ed. Musya Glants and Joyce Stetson Toomre (Bloomington, Indiana: Indiana University Press, 1997), 33.

7. Letter to Mrs. Robert Wilmot, *The Russian Journals*, 75.

8. Claire Le Corbellier, "Figures to Adorn the Middle of the Desert," in *Figures from Life* (St. Petersburg, Florida: Museum of Fine Arts, 1992), 9. For more on dessert centerpieces, see *The Edible Monument: The Art of Food for Festivals* (Malibu, California: A Getty Research Institute Exhibition, 2000).

9. Lydia Liackhova, "In a Porcelain Mirror: Reflections of Russia from Peter I to Empress Elizabeth," in *Fragile Diplomacy: Meissen Porcelain for European Courts ca. 1710–1763*, ed. Maureen Cassidy-Geiger (New Haven: Yale University Press, 2007), 72, 76–77 for illustrations. The service was actually started before the marriage was announced, but it appears that Augustus III decided to use this occasion to give the gift to Elizabeth.

10. *Kamerfur'erskii tseremonial'nyi zhurnal* (hereafter *KTZ*) 1772 (Saint Petersburg, 1853–1903), 113.

11. *KTZ*, 1772, 113.

12. Richard Wortman, *Scenarios of Power: Myth and Ceremony in Russian Monarchy, Vol. I* (Princeton: Princeton University Press, 1995 and 2000), 136.

13. [Baron Nikolai von Wolff], *Imperatorskii farforovyi zavod 1744–1904* (St. Petersburg: Izdanie Upravleniia imperatorskimi zavodami, 1906), 87–88, 108–109.

14. See Karen L. Kettering, "The Russian porcelain figure in the eighteenth and nineteenth centuries," in *The Magazine Antiques* March, 2003, 114–119.

15. Quoted in Rosalind Savill, "Cameo Fever: Six Pieces from the Sèvres Porcelain Dinner Service made for Catherine II of Russia," *Apollo* 116, no. 249 (November 1982), 304.

16. [Von Wolff], 139.

17. [Von Wolff], 79–80.

18. Wortman, Vol. 1, 89.

19. Ibid.

20. *KTZ*, 1784, 487.

21. *KTZ*, 1799, 962.

22. For more on this trip, see Anne Odom, "Souvenirs from Catherine's Crimean Tour, "The Post, vol. 5, no.1, (Spring, 1998), 7–12. Troinitskii also argues that the service was made for this trip. Sergei Troinitskii, "Galereia farfora imperatorskogo ermitazha," *Starye gody* (October 1911), 11.

23. M. G. Voronov, *Gavriil Ignat'evich Kozlov: Zhizn' i tvorchestvo* (Leningrad: "Khudozhnik RSFSR," 1982), 67–74 and Nataliia Sipovskaia, "Ordenskie servizy," *Pinakoteka* No. 5 (Moscow) 1998, 16–31.

24. *KTZ*, 30 August 1797, 827.

25. RGIA (Russian State Historical Archive, St. Petersburg), *fond* 469, *opis* 14, *delo* 200, list 84.

26. For more on the Cabinet and dowry services, see Anne Odom, "The Cabinet Service and its Variants," *The Post* vol.1, no. 2 (Spring 1994), 5–12.

27. See Odom, 1999, for an example, 36.

28. See W. Baer, "Veduta Painting on Porcelain in the Eighteenth Century," in *Along the Royal Road: Berlin and Potsdam, 1815–1848* (New York: The Bard Graduate Center in the Decorative Arts, 1993), 55, and Anne Odom "Of Tea and Tragedy: The Story of a Vienna Tea and Coffee Set," *Bulletin of the Detroit Institute of Arts*, Vol.73, No. ½ (1999), 30–41.

29. RGIA, *fond* 516, *opis* 1 (120/2322), *delo* 8, list 85, 1826. *Kamerfur'erskii tsereonial'nyi zhurnal'*. Coronation of Nicholas I, August 22. After 1817 KTZ exists only in archival form.

30. For more about Solntsev's designs and their impact on the decorative arts, see Anne Odom, "A Revolution in Russian Design: Solntsev and the Decorative Arts," in *Visualizing Russia: Fedor Solntsev and Crafting a National Past*, ed. Cynthyia Hyla Whittaker (Leiden: Brill, 2010), 41–59.

31. RGIA, *fond* 503, *opis* 2, *delo* 821, 1836, list 18.

32. Ibid, list 114.

33. RGIA, *fond* 503, *opis* 2, *delo* 483, list 21 and 23.

34. [Von Wolff], 199, 216.

35. Count Paul Vassili, *Behind the Veil at the Russian Court* (New York: Joan Lane Company, 1914), 157.

36. W. A. L. Seaman and J. R. Sewall, eds., *Russian Journal of Lady Londonderry 1836–1837* (London: John Murray, 1973), 111.

GLOSSARY

Cartouche/Reserves
An oval or oblong enclosing an image.

Cavetto
Sunken center of a flat dish, plate or soup plate.

Charger
Larger decorative plates.

Charka
A drinking vessel used in Russia, meaning vodka or tot cup.

Cipher
A combination of symbolic letters; especially the interwoven initials of a name (monograph).

Ciselé
Metallic painting having a chased or chiseled appearance.

Compotier/Compote:
A dish for holding compotes, fruit, etc.

En grisaille
A term for paintings executed entirely in monochrome or near-monochrome, usually in shades of grey.

Ewer
A vase-shaped pitcher, often decorated, with a base and a flaring spout.

Finial
A decorative end piece knob.

Hard-paste porcelain
Porcelain including a mixture of kaolin, feldspar and quartz, fired at very high temperatures.

Salt
A dish for salt. Salt would be provided to diners in open dishes and applied with a small spoon, rather than in a shaker familiar to contemporary diners, as without anti-caking additives, salt can clump.

Soft-paste porcelain
The precursor to hard-paste porcelain, developed at various European factories such as Sèvres. The earliest formulations were mixtures of clay and ground-up glass (frit). These wares were not yet true or hard-paste porcelain as they were not hard and vitrified by firing kaolin clay at high temperatures.

BIOGRAPHY: KATHLEEN DURDIN

Growing up in central Florida in the 1960s, Kathleen Durdin first became fascinated in Russian history and decorative arts by reading Grand Duchess Marie's book, *The Education of a Princess,* and collecting the magazine advertisements that featured the Forbes Faberge collection.

Ms. Durdin graduated from the College of William & Mary, where she majored in accounting and took extensive coursework in art history. She continues to be active in both the business and art programs at William & Mary—Ms. Durdin is both on the Muscarelle Museum of Art Board of Directors and is Chairperson of the Business Partners Board of the Mason School of Business Undergraduate Program. In 2010, Ms. Durdin was recognized for her outstanding volunteer service to the program.

Ms. Durdin has spent more than 30 years in the consulting industry as a litigation and management consultant with Navigant. She is currently a Director of Learning and Professional Development and Chief Diversity Officer of Navigant.

Since graduating, Ms. Durdin continued her interest in art, with a particular focus on decorative arts. She has been a passionate collector for more than 20 years, focusing on Continental porcelain and other decorative arts. She bought her first piece of Faberge in 1998 (the Grand Duke Nicholas cigarette case included in the exhibition). In 2000, she started collecting Russian Imperial porcelain with the plate from the *Derzhava,* also included in the exhibition. Since that time, with the assistance of John Atzbach, and a combination of diligence and luck, she has developed one of the finest collections of Russian Imperial porcelain in the United States, some of which is included in *The Tsars' Cabinet* exhibition. The collection has been developed with a particular focus on items from the eighteenth century, as well as pieces from major services of the nineteenth century. In addition, pieces made outside Russia for the Imperial court, such as items from the Frog Service by Wedgwood, the Cameo Service by Sèvres, and various Berlin and Meissen services, are also well represented.

In addition to her professional activities and collecting, Ms. Durdin is a noted, nationally exhibited watercolor artist. In 2012, she will be President of Florida Watercolor Society, the largest state based watercolor society in the United States. She is also active in the historic preservation of her neighborhood, and is Treasurer of her neighborhood association.

lacy stripes scarf

Easy

MATERIALS

Yarn
RED HEART® Heart & Sole®, 1¾oz/50g balls, each approx 187yd/171m (wool/nylon)
- 4 balls in 3313 Ivory

Needles
- One pair size 5 (3.75mm) needles, *or size to obtain gauge*

Notions
- Stitch markers
- Yarn needle

FINISHED MEASUREMENTS
Width 15"/38cm
Length 59"/150cm

GAUGE
22 sts = 4"/10cm; 32 rows = 4"/10cm over Lace Pattern using size 5 (3.75mm) needles.
CHECK YOUR GAUGE. Use any size needles to obtain the gauge

SHAWL
Cast on 80 sts.

Seed Stitch Border
Row 1 (Wrong Side) *K1, p1; repeat from * across.
Row 2 *P1, k1; repeat from * across.
Repeat rows 1 and 2 once more.

Begin Lace Pattern
Row 1 (Wrong Side) [K1, p1] twice (for Seed st border), pm, p to last 4 sts, pm, [k1, p1] twice (for Seed st border).
Row 2 [P1, k1] twice, sm, *yo, k2, k2tog, k2; repeat from * to marker, sm, [p1, k1] twice.
Row 3 [K1, p1] twice, sm, p to marker, sm, [k1, p1] twice.
Row 4 [P1, k1] twice, sm, *k2, k2tog, k2, yo; repeat from * to marker, sm, [p1, k1] twice.
Row 5 Repeat Row 3.
Repeat Rows 2–5 until piece measures 58½"/148.5cm from beginning, end with a Wrong Side row.

Seed Stitch Border
Row 1 (Right Side) *P1, k1; repeat from * across.
Row 2 *K1, p1; repeat from * across.
Repeat rows 1 and 2 once more.
Bind off all sts.

FINISHING
Weave in loose ends. Block to finished measurements.•

brighten my day shawl

Easy

MATERIALS

Yarn
RED HEART® Super Saver™, 7oz/198g balls, each approx 364yd/333m (acrylic) 4
- 1 ball in 312 Black (A)

RED HEART® Super Saver Stripes™, 5oz/141g balls, each approx 236yd/215m (acrylic) 4
- 1 ball in 4960 Polo Stripe (B)

Needles
- One pair size 10 (6mm) needles, *or size to obtain gauge*

FINISHED MEASUREMENTS

Width (along top edge) 70"/178cm
Height (at longest point) 18"/46cm

GAUGE

14 sts = 4"/10cm; 28 rows = 4"/10cm in Garter Stitch using size 10 (6mm) needles. *CHECK YOUR GAUGE. Use any size needles to obtain the gauge.*

NOTES

1) Shawl is worked in Garter Stitch (knit every row).
2) Carry A and B without cutting between stripes.

SHAWL

With A, cast on 5 sts. Knit 1 row.
Join B, knit 2 rows.
Row 1 (Right Side) With A, k to last 2 sts, kfb, k1—1 st increased.
Row 2 With A, knit
Rows 3 and 4 With B, knit.
Rep rows 1–4 until there are 60 sts, ending after a row 4.
Begin to decrease on next A stripe as follows:
Row 5 (Right Side) With A, k to last 3 sts, k2tog, k1—1 st decreased.
Row 6 With A, knit.
Rows 7 and 8 With B, knit.
Repeat rows 5–8 until 5 sts remain, ending after row 6.
Bind off all stitches loosely.

FINISHING

Weave in loose ends. Block to finished measurements.•

stunning lace scarf

NOTE
Pattern can be worked following written instructions or chart.

SCARF
Cast on 43 sts.
Row 1 (Right Side) K1, k2tog, *k4, yo, k1, yo**, S2KP; repeat from * 4 times, ending last repeat at **, SKP, k1.
Row 2 and all even rows Purl.
Row 3 K1, k2tog, *k3, yo, k1, yo, k1**, S2KP; repeat from * 4 times, ending last repeat at **, SKP, k1.
Row 5 K1, k2tog, *k2, yo, k1, yo, k2**, S2KP; repeat from * 4 times, ending last repeat at **, SKP, k1.
Row 7 K1, k2tog, *k1, yo, k1, yo, k3**, S2KP; repeat from * 4 times, ending last repeat at **, SKP, k1.
Row 9 K1, k2tog, *yo, k1, yo, k4**, S2KP; repeat from * 4 times, ending last repeat at **, SKP, k1.
Row 11 Repeat Row 7.
Row 13 Repeat Row 5.
Row 15 Repeat Row 3.
Row 16 Purl.
Repeat Rows 1–16 until scarf measures 75"/190cm from cast-on edge, ending with Row 2.
Bind off all sts.

FINISHING
Weave in loose ends. Block to finished measurements.•

Intermediate

MATERIALS
Yarn
RED HEART® Dreamy™, 8.8oz/250g balls, each approx 466yd/426m (acrylic)
• 1 ball in 8512 Aqua

Needles
• One pair size 10½ (6.5mm) needles, *or size to obtain gauge*

FINISHED MEASUREMENTS
Width 12"/30cm
Length 75"/190cm

GAUGE
15 sts = 4"/10cm; 1 pattern repeat = 4"/10cm using size 10½ (6.5mm) needles.
CHECK YOUR GAUGE. Use any size needles to obtain the gauge.

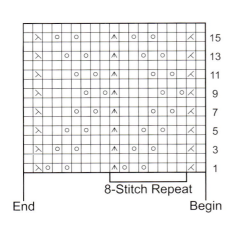

Stitch Key
☐ = K on RS, p on WS
⊠ = K2tog
⋀ = S2kp
⊠ = Skp
○ = Yo

ribbed slit shawl

Easy

MATERIALS
Yarn
RED HEART® Soft®, 5oz/141g balls, each approx 256yd/234m (acrylic) (4)
• 1 (1, 2) balls in 4608 Wine

Needles
• One size 8 (5mm) circular needle, 24"/61cm long, *or size to obtain gauge*
• One pair sizes 8 (5mm) needle

Notions
• One size H-8 (5mm) crochet hook
• 40"/101.5cm length of contrasting scrap yarn

SIZES
Small (Medium, Large).

FINISHED MEASUREMENTS
Width 18 (22, 26)"/46 (56, 66)cm
Length 65 (75, 85)"/165 (190.5, 216)cm

GAUGE
20 sts = 4"/10cm; 24 rows = 4"/10cm in k3, p2 rib using size 8 (5mm) needles. *CHECK YOUR GAUGE. Use any size needles to obtain the gauge.*

NOTES
1) Shawl is worked back and forth in rows. Circular needle is used to accommodate large number of stitches. Do *not* join.
2) Contrasting yarn is used as a marker for placement of keyhole. Use as a guide when picking up stitches to make slit.
3) Slip stitches purlwise.

SHAWL
With circular needle, cast on 90 (110, 130) sts.
Row 1 (Wrong Side) Slip 1, p3, k2, *p3, k2; repeat from * to last 4 sts, p3, slip 1.
Row 2 K4, p2, *k3, p2; repeat from * to last 4 sts, k4.
Repeat Rows 1 and 2 until shawl measures 5 (7, 9)"/12.7 (18, 23)cm from beginning, ending with a Wrong Side row.
Next Row Keeping in pattern, work across first 36 (46, 56) sts; work across next 23 stitches holding contrasting yarn and working yarn together; drop contrasting yarn and work to end.
Continue in working yarn and pattern as established until shawl measures 11 (14, 17)"/28 (35.5, 43) cm from beginning, ending with a Wrong Side row. Cut yarn.

Slit
With crochet hook, and using contrasting yarn as a guide, hold yarn to Wrong Side of work and pull 1 st through the center of each of 23 sts marked for slit. Place sts on straight knitting needle, and attach yarn to Right Side—23 sts.
Row 1 (Right Side) *K3, p2; repeat from * to last 3 sts, k3.
Row 2 *P3, k2; repeat from * to last 3 sts, p3.
Repeat Rows 1 and 2 until piece measures 6 (7, 8)"/15 (18, 20)cm, ending with a Wrong Side row. Cut yarn.

Join Slit to Shawl
Attach yarn to Right Side of sts waiting on circular needle for shawl, keeping in pattern, work across first 36 (46, 56) sts; holding needles parallel with each other so that needle holding slit sts is in front of needle holding shawl sts, work the first sts from each needle together until all 23 sts of slit have been worked, continue across remaining 31 (41 51) sts of shawl—90 (110, 130) sts.
Work in pattern as established until shawl measures 65 (75, 85)"/165 (190.5, 216)cm from beginning, ending with a Wrong Side row.
Bind of all stitches.

FINISHING
Weave in loose ends. Remove contrasting yarn.•

voyager poncho

Easy

MATERIALS

Yarn
RED HEART® Heart & Sole®, 1¾oz/50g balls, each approx 187yd/171m (wool/nylon)
- 5 balls in 3933 Skyscraper

Needles
- One size 4 (3.5mm) circular needle, 29"/73.5cm long, *or size to obtain gauge*
- One size 4 (3.5mm) needle, for three-needle bind-off

Notions
- Stitch markers
- Yarn needle

FINISHED MEASUREMENTS

Width 60"/152cm
Length 19"/48cm

GAUGE

24 sts = 4"/10cm; 32 rows = 4"/10cm, over St st, before blocking, using size 4 (3.5mm) needle.
CHECK YOUR GAUGE. Use any size needle to obtain the gauge.

SEED STITCH

Row 1 *K1, p1, repeat from * across row.
Row 2 *P1, k1, repeat from * across row.
Repeat Rows 1–2 for Seed Stitch.

NOTE

Poncho is worked back and forth in rows. Circular needle is used to accommodate large number of stitches. Do *not* join.

PONCHO

Cast on 310 sts.
Work in Seed Stitch until piece measures 2"/5cm from cast-on edge.
Row 1 (Right Side) Work first 12 sts in Seed Stitch, pm, K96 sts, pm, work Chart over next 23 sts, pm, k48, pm, work Chart over next 23 sts, pm, k96, pm, work last 12 sts in Seed Stitch—310 sts.
Row 2 Work in Seed Stitch to first marker, sm, p to last marker, sm, work remaining sts in Seed Stitch.
Repeat Rows 1 and 2, continue to work Chart over stitches indicated until piece measures 18"/46cm from cast-on edge. End with a Wrong Side row.
Next Row (Right Side) Work first 12 sts in Seed Stitch, k84 sts, bind off next 118 sts, k84 sts to last marker, work remaining sts in Seed Stitch—192 sts.

FINISHING

With 192 sts still on needle, place 96 sts on each needle. Hold Right Sides of work together and work three-needle bind-off on remaining sts as follows: Put right needle through first st on front needle, then through first st on back needle, knit them together in the usual manner. *Knit together first st on front and back needles in the same way. Two sts now are on right needle. Lift right-most st over the last st knit and off the needle—one st now bound off. Repeat from * until all sts are bound off.

Weave in loose ends. Block to finished measurements.•

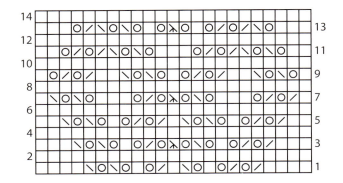

zigzaggy scarf

Easy

MATERIALS
Yarn
RED HEART® Super Saver®, 7oz/198g skeins, each approx 364yd/333m (acrylic)
• 2 skeins in 512 Turqua

Needles
• One pair size 8 (5mm) needles, *or size to obtain gauge*

Notions
• Yarn needle

FINISHED MEASUREMENTS
Width 7"/18cm
Length (excluding fringe) 72"/183cm

GAUGE
19 sts = 4"/10cm; 23 rows = 4"/10cm over Right Diagonal Stitch using size 8 (5mm) needles.
CHECK YOUR GAUGE. Use any size needles to obtain the gauge given.

RIGHT DIAGONAL STITCH
(multiple of 6 sts plus 3)
Row 1 (Right Side) K3, *slip 3 with yarn in front, k3; repeat from * across.
Row 2 P4, *slip 3 with yarn in back, p3; repeat from * to last 5 sts, slip 3 with yarn in back, p2.
Row 3 K1, *slip 3 with yarn in front, k3; repeat from * to last 2 sts, k2.
Row 4 P6, *slip 3 with yarn in back, p3; repeat from * to last 3 sts, p3.
Row 5 K5, *slip 3 with yarn in front, k3; repeat from * to last 4 sts, slip 3 with yarn in front, k1.
Row 6 P2, *slip 3 with yarn in back, p3; repeat from * to last st, p1.
Repeat Rows 1–6 for Right Diagonal Stitch.

LEFT DIAGONAL STITCH
(multiple of 6 sts plus 3)
Row 1 (Right Side) K3, *slip 3 with yarn in front, k3; repeat from * across.
Row 2 P2, *slip 3 with yarn in back, p3; repeat from * to last st, p1.
Row 3 K5, *slip 3 with yarn in front, k3; repeat from * to last 4 sts, slip 3 with yarn in front, k1.
Row 4 P6, *slip 3 with yarn in back, p3; repeat from * to last 3 sts, p3.
Row 5 K1, *slip 3 with yarn in front, k3; repeat from * to last 2 sts, k2.
Row 6 P4, *slip 3 with yarn in back, p3; repeat from * to last 5 sts, slip 3 with yarn in back, p2.
Repeat Rows 1–6 for Left Diagonal Stitch.

NOTE
Stitch patterns will create a ruffled edge along the side of your work.

SCARF
Cast on 33 sts.
*Work Rows 1–6 of the Right Diagonal Stitch 8 times.
Work Rows 1–6 of the Left Diagonal Stitch 8 times.
Repeat from * until work measures 72"/183cm, end after completing Row 6 of either stitch.
Bind off.

FINISHING
Weave in loose ends. Block to finished measurements.

Fringe
Cut sixty-six 12"/30.5cm strands of yarn. *Fold one strand in half to form a loop. With Right Side facing, insert loop from Right Side to Wrong Side at edge st. Thread fringe tails through loop and secure knot; repeat from * for each edge st across for a total of 33 strands of fringe. Repeat for each st across opposite edge. Trim fringe evenly.•

statement scarf

Easy

MATERIALS

Yarn
RED HEART® Soft Essentials™, 5oz/140g balls, each approx 131yd/120m (acrylic) 5
- 5 balls in 7103 Cream

Needles
- One pair size 11 (8mm) needles, *or size to obtain gauge*

Notions
- One size K-10½ (6.5mm) crochet hook (optional)
- Yarn needle

FINISHED MEASUREMENTS
Width 14"/35.5cm
Length 96"/244cm

GAUGE
15 sts = 4"/10cm; 16 rows = 4"/10cm in 3x2 Rib, slightly stretched, using size 11 (8mm) needles.
CHECK YOUR GAUGE. Use any size needles to obtain the gauge.

SCARF
Cast on 45 sts.
Row 1 (Right Side) Slip 1, *k3, p2; repeat from * to last 4 sts, k4.
Row 2 Slip 1, p3, *k2, p3; repeat from * to last st, k1.
Repeat Rows 1 and 2 for 3x2 Rib until piece measures 40½"/103cm from cast-on, ending with a Right Side row.

Armhole Row 1 (Wrong Side) Slip 1, p3, k2, p3, bind off 26, p3, k2, p3, k1.
Armhole Row 2 Slip 1, k3, p2, k3, cast on 26, k3, p2, k4.
Armhole Row 3 Slip 1, p3, *k2, p3; repeat from * to last st, k1.

Repeat Rows 1 and 2 for 3x2 Rib as before until piece measures 55"/140cm from cast-on, ending with a Right Side row.

Repeat Armhole Rows.

Repeat Rows 1 and 2 for 3x2 Rib as before until piece measures 96"/244cm from cast-on, ending with a Wrong Side row.
Bind off all stitches.

FINISHING
Weave in loose ends.
If desired, using crochet hook, work 1 row of single crochet around armhole openings.•

eight-hour shawl

Easy

MATERIALS
Yarn
RED HEART® Soft®, 5oz/141g balls, each approx 256yd/234m (acrylic)
• 2 balls in 9779 Berry

Needles
• One pair size 10½ (6.5mm) needles, *or size to obtain gauge*

FINISHED MEASUREMENTS
Width 16"/40.5cm
Length 56"/142cm

GAUGE
11 sts = 4"/10cm; 10 rows = 4"/10cm in Ridged Stitch using size 10½ (6.5mm) needles.
CHECK YOUR GAUGE. Use any size needles to obtain the gauge.

RIDGED STITCH
(multiple of 4 sts plus 2)
Row 1 (Wrong Side) Knit.
Row 2 Knit.
Row 3 K2, *p2, k2; repeat from * to end.
Row 4 P2, *k2, p2; repeat from * to end.
Repeat Rows 1–4 for Ridged Stitch.

SCARF
Cast on 16 sts.
Knit 2 rows.
Row 1 (Wrong Side) K1 (edge st), beginning with Row 1, work Ridged Stitch over center 14 sts, k1 (edge st).
Keeping first and last st in Garter Stitch (knit every row) and center 14 sts in Ridged Stitch, work until piece measures 95"/241cm from beginning, ending with Row 2 of Ridged Stitch.
Knit 2 rows.
Bind off knitwise.

FINISHING
Weave in loose ends. Block to finished measurements.•

honeycomb stitch scarf

Easy

MATERIALS
Yarn
RED HEART® Comfort®, 16oz/454g balls, each approx 867yd/792m (acrylic)
• 1 ball in 3240 Cream

Needles
• One pair size 10½ (6.5mm) needles, *or size to obtain gauge*

FINISHED MEASUREMENTS
Width 17"/43cm
Length 72"/183cm

GAUGE
18 sts = 4"/10cm; 21 rows = 4"/10cm in Honeycomb Stitch Pattern using size 10½ (6.5mm) needles.
CHECK YOUR GAUGE. Use any size needles to obtain the gauge.

SPECIAL ABBREVIATIONS
C2F (Cross 2 Front) Knit into front of 2nd st on needle, then knit into first st, slip both sts off needle at the same time.
C2B (Cross 2 Back) Knit into back of 2nd st on needle, knit first st, slip both sts off needle at the same time.

HONEYCOMB STITCH PATTERN
(multiple of 4 sts)
Row 1 (Right Side) *C2F, C2B; repeat from * to end.
Row 2 Purl.
Row 3 *C2B, C2F; repeat from * to end.
Row 4 Purl.
Repeat Rows 1–4 for Honeycomb Stitch Pattern.

SCARF
Cast on 78 sts.
Work in Garter Stitch (knit every row) for 1"/2.5cm, ending with a Wrong Side row.
Next row (Right Side) Work first 5 sts in Garter Stitch, work center 68 sts in Honeycomb Stitch Pattern, work last 5 sts in Garter Stitch.
Continue working in established pattern until scarf measures 71"/180cm from beginning.
Work in Garter Stitch for 1"/2.5cm.
Bind off all stitches.

FINISHING
Weave in loose ends. Block to finished measurements.•

lacy ridges shawl

MATERIALS

Yarn
RED HEART® Super Saver Ombre™, 10oz/283g skeins, each approx 482yd/440m (acrylic)
- 1 skein in 3961 Scuba

Needles
- One size 8 (5mm) circular needle, 36"/91cm long, *or size to obtain gauge*

Notions
- Stitch markers
- Yarn needle

FINISHED MEASUREMENTS

Width (at widest point) 72"/183cm
Length (at longest point) 24"/61cm

GAUGE

15 sts = 4"/10cm; 22 rows = 4"/10cm in Eyelet Stripe Stitch using size 8 (5mm) needle.
CHECK YOUR GAUGE. *Use any size needle to obtain the gauge.*

NOTE

Shawl is worked back and forth in rows. Circular needle is used to accommodate large number of stitches. Do *not* join.

EYELET STRIPE STITCH

(over an odd number of sts)
Row 1 (Right Side) Knit.
Row 2 Purl.
Rows 3–6 Rep rows 1 and 2 twice.
Row 7 K1, [yo, k2tog] to end.
Row 8 Purl.
Rep rows 1–8 for Eyelet Stripe Stitch.

SHAWL

Cast on 5 sts.
Row 1 (Right Side) K1, yo, k1, yo, pm, k1, pm, yo, k1, yo, k1—9 sts.
Row 2 Knit.
Row 3 K1, yo, k to marker, yo, sm, k1, sm, yo, k to last st, yo, k1—13 sts.
Row 4 Knit.
Rows 5–10 Repeat Rows 3 and 4 three more times—25 sts on last row worked.
Row 11 K1, yo, k to marker, yo, sm, k1, sm, yo, k to last st, yo, k1—29 sts.
Row 12 K1, p to last st, k1.
Rows 13–16 Repeat Rows 11 and 12 two more times—37 sts on last row worked.
Row 17 (Right Side) K1, yo, k1, [yo, k2tog] to marker, yo, sm, k1, sm, [yo, k2tog] to last 2 sts, yo, k1, yo, k1—41 sts.
Row 18 Repeat Row 12.
Repeat Rows 11–18 until piece measures 23½"/60cm from beginning and 269 sts are on last row worked, end with Row 11.
Next row (Wrong Side) Knit.
Next row K1, yo, k to last st, yo, k1—271 sts.
Bind off knitwise on Wrong Side.

FINISHING

Weave in loose ends.
To block, pin piece out to measurements and spray with water. Leave to dry.•

crescent shawl

Easy

MATERIALS
Yarn
RED HEART® Hopscotch, 4oz/113g balls, each approx 210yd/193m (acrylic) (4)
• 2 balls in 7958 Kickball

Needles
• One size 8 (5mm) circular needle, 36"/91cm long, *or size to obtain gauge*

Notions
• Removable stitch marker (optional)
• Yarn needle

FINISHED MEASUREMENTS
Width 60"/152.5cm
Length (at longest point) 15"/38cm

GAUGE
16 sts = 4"/10cm; 32 rows = 4"/10cm in garter st using size 8 (5mm) needle. *CHECK YOUR GAUGE. Use any size needles to obtain the gauge.*

SPECIAL ABBREVIATIONS
2yo Yarn over twice around needle.
K2tbl Knit 2 stitches together through the back loop—1 stitch decreased.
KyoK [K1, yo, k1] into same stitch—2 stitches increased.

NOTES
1) To make top edge of shawl stretchy, at beginning of every row, knit first st, place it back onto left hand needle, knit it again, then continue row as instructed.
2) Shawl is worked back and forth in rows. Circular needle is used to accommodate large number of stitches. Do *not* join.
3) If helpful, mark Right Side of shawl with stitch marker.

SHAWL
Cast on 5 sts.
Row 1 Knit.
Row 2 (Right Side) K1, kfb, k1, kfb, k1—7 sts.
Row 3 K2, yo, k3, yo, k2—9 sts.
Row 4 K3, KyoK, k to last 4 sts, KyoK, k3—4 sts increased.
Row 5 K3, yo, k to last 3 sts, yo, k3—2 sts increased.
Repeat Rows 4 and 5 forty-five more times—285 sts.
Next row K3, KyoK, *K2tog, 2yo; repeat from * to last 5 sts, k1, KyoK, k3.
Next row K3, yo, k to last 3 sts (knitting once into each 2yo and dropping extra wrap), yo, k3.
Repeat Rows 4 and 5 two more times.
Bind off all sts follows:
Knit first st. *knit next st, slip 2 sts from right needle to left needle, K2tbl (1 st remains on the right needle). Repeat from * across to bind off all sts.

FINISHING
Weave in loose ends. Block to finished measurements.•

cozy shoulders poncho

●●● Intermediate

MATERIALS

Yarn
RED HEART® With Love® Stripes™, 5oz/141g balls, each approx 223yd/204 (acrylic)
- 2 balls in 1975 Sandbar Stripe

Needles
- One size 10½ (6.5mm) circular needle, 24"/60cm long, *or size to obtain gauge*

Notions
- Stitch marker
- Yarn needle

FINISHED MEASUREMENTS
Circumference 45"/114cm
Length 16½"/42cm

GAUGE
14 sts = 4"/10cm; 24 rows = 4"/10cm in Welt st using size 10½ (6.5mm) needle. *CHECK YOUR GAUGE. Use any size needles to obtain the gauge.*

STRETCHY BIND-OFF
K2, *insert left needle into front of 2 sts on right needle (from the left), k2tog through the back loop, k1; repeat from * around until all sts have been bound off. Fasten off last stitch.

WELT STITCH
(worked in the round over any number of stitches)
Rounds 1–3 Knit.
Rounds 4–6 Purl.
Repeat Rounds 1–6 for Welt st.

PONCHO
Cast on 156 sts. Join to work in rounds, taking care not to twist sts. Place marker for beginning of round.
Beginning with Round 1, repeat Rounds 1–6 for Welt st until piece measures 8"/20.5cm from beginning, ending with Round 6.

Shape Shoulders
Decrease Round (K2, k2tog) around—117 sts.
Continue in Welt st until piece measures 12"/30.5cm from beginning, ending with Round 6.
Decrease Round (K1, k2tog) around—78 sts.
Continue in Welt st until piece measures 16½"/42cm from beginning, ending with Round 3.
Bind off using Stretchy Bind-Off method.

FINISHING
Weave in loose ends. Block lightly, if desired.●

reverse sand stitch scarf

Easy

MATERIALS

Yarn
RED HEART® Super Saver Chunky™,
5oz/141g skeins, each approx
173yd/158m (acrylic)
• 2 skeins in 259 Flamingo

Needles
• One pair size 11 (8mm) needles, *or size to obtain gauge*

Notions
• One size K-10½ (6.5mm) crochet hook
• Yarn needle

FINISHED MEASUREMENTS
Width 7"/18cm
Length (excluding fringe) 76"/193cm

GAUGE
11 sts = 4"/10cm; 18 rows = 4"/10cm in Reverse Sand Stitch using size 11 (8mm) needles.
CHECK YOUR GAUGE. Use any size needles to obtain the gauge.

REVERSE SAND STITCH
(over even number of stitches)
Row 1 (Right Side) Knit.
Row 2 *K1, p1; repeat from * to end of row.
Row 3 Knit.
Row 4 *P1, k1; repeat from * to end of row.
Repeat Rows 1–4 for Reverse Sand Stitch.

NOTE
Knit first and last stitch of every row for edge st.

SCARF
Cast on 20 stitches.
Set up pattern as follows:
K1, work Row 1 of Reverse Sand Stitch to last stitch, k1.
Continuing to knit the first and last stitch of every row and Reverse Sand st over center 18 stitches, work until scarf measures 76"/193cm, ending with a Wrong Side row.
Bind off knitwise.

FINISHING
Weave in loose ends. Block to finished measurements.

Fringe
Cut yarn into sixty 12"/30.5cm lengths. Hold 3 strands of yarn together and fold in half, forming a loop at one end. *Insert crochet hook into corner of one short edge of scarf and place loop on hook. Draw loop through, insert ends through loop and pull to tighten; repeat from * to attach a total of 10 fringes evenly across edge. Repeat for other short edge of scarf. Trim fringe evenly.•

laid-back shawl

Easy

MATERIALS

Yarn
RED HEART® Heart & Sole®, 1¾oz/50g balls, each approx 187yd/171m (wool/nylon)
• 2 balls in 3932 Denimy

Needles
• One pair size 10 (6mm) needles, *or size to obtain gauges*

FINISHED MEASUREMENTS
Width 18"/45.5cm
Length 58"/147.5cm

GAUGES
16 sts = 4"/10cm in Open Mesh pattern, before blocking; 12 sts = 4"/10cm in Open Mesh pattern, after blocking, using size 19 (6mm) needles.
CHECK YOUR GAUGES. Use any size needles to obtain the gauges.

NOTE
Open Mesh Pattern can be worked from written instructions or chart.

SHAWL
Cast on 55 sts.
Begin Open Mesh Pattern
Row 1 (Right Side) K2, *yo, SK2P, yo, k1; repeat from * to last st, k1.
Row 2 Purl.
Row 3 K1, k2tog, *yo, k1, yo, SK2P; repeat from * to last 4 sts, yo, k1, yo, ssk, k1.
Row 4 Purl.
Repeat Rows 1–4 until piece measures about 58"/147.5cm from beginning. Bind off loosely.

FINISHING
Weave in loose ends. Block to finished measurements.•

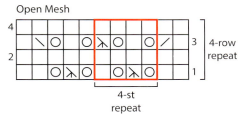

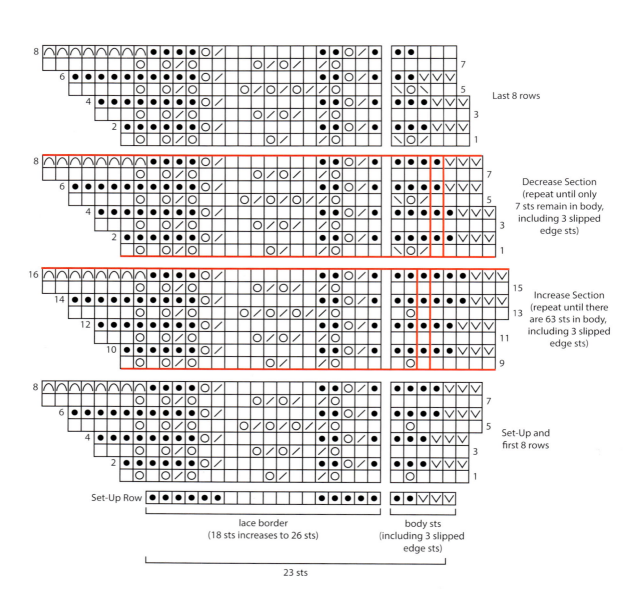

lace-trimmed shawl

Row 14 K10, yo, k2tog, p7, k2, yo, k2tog, k1, sm, k to last 3 sts, bring yarn between needles to front, slip last 3 sts.
Row 15 K to marker, sm, k3, yo, k2tog, k1, [k2tog, yo] twice, k4, yo, k2tog, [yo, k1] twice, k6—35 sts (26 sts in lace border, 9 sts in body).
Row 16 Bind off 8 sts (1 st on right needle when bind-off complete), k3, yo, k2tog, p7, k2, yo, k2tog, k1, sm, k to last 3 sts, bring yarn between needles to front, slip last 3 sts—27 sts (18 sts in lace border, 9 sts in body).
Repeat these 8 Increase Section rows 27 more times; ending with a Row 16—81 sts (18 sts in lace border, 63 sts in body).

Decrease Section
Row 1 (Right Side) K to 4 sts before marker, k2tog, yo, ssk, sm, k3, yo, k2tog, k2, k2tog, yo, k5, yo, k2tog, [yo, k1] twice—82 sts (20 sts in lace border, 62 sts in body).
Row 2 K6, yo, k2tog, p7, k2, yo, k2tog, k1, sm, k to last 3 sts, bring yarn between needles to front, slip last 3 sts.
Row 3 K to marker, sm, k3, yo, k2tog, k1, [k2tog, yo] twice, k4, yo, k2tog, [yo, k1] twice, k2—84 sts (22 sts in lace border, 62 sts in body).
Row 4 K8, yo, k2tog, p7, k2, yo, k2tog, k1, sm, k to last 3 sts, bring yarn between needles to front, slip last 3 sts.
Row 5 K to 4 sts before marker, k2tog, yo, ssk, sm, k3, yo, k2tog, [k2tog, yo] 3 times, k3, yo, k2tog, [yo, k1] twice, k4—85 sts (24 sts in lace border, 61 sts in body).
Row 6 K10, yo, k2tog, p7, k2, yo, k2tog, k1, sm, k to last 3 sts, bring yarn between needles to front, slip last 3 sts.
Row 7 K to marker, sm, k3, yo, k2tog, k1, [k2tog, yo] twice, k4, yo, k2tog, [yo, k1] twice, k6—87 sts (26 sts in lace border, 61 sts in body).

Row 8 Bind off 8 sts (1 st on right needle when bind-off complete), k3, yo, k2tog, p7, k2, yo, k2tog, k1, sm, k to last 3 sts, bring yarn between needles to front, slip last 3 sts—79 sts (18 sts in lace border, 61 sts in body)
Repeat these 8 Decrease Section rows 27 more times; ending with a Row 8—25 sts (18 sts in lace border, 7 sts in body).

Last 8 Rows
Row 1 (Right Side) K to 4 sts before marker, k2tog, yo, ssk, sm, k3, yo, k2tog, k2, k2tog, yo, k5, yo, k2tog, [yo, k1] twice—26 sts (20 sts in lace border, 6 sts in body).
Row 2 K6, yo, k2tog, p7, k2, yo, k2tog, k1, sm, k3, bring yarn between needles to front, slip last 3 sts.
Row 3 K6, sm, k3, yo, k2tog, k1, [k2tog, yo] twice, k4, yo, k2tog, [yo, k1] twice, k2—28 sts (22 sts in lace border, 6 sts in body).
Row 4 K8, yo, k2tog, p7, k2, yo, k2tog, k1, sm, k3, bring yarn between needles to front, slip last 3 sts.
Row 5 K2, ssk, yo, ssk, sm, k3, yo, k2tog, [k2tog, yo] 3 times, k3, yo, k2tog, [yo, k1] twice, k4—29 sts (24 sts in lace border, 5 sts in body).
Row 6 K10, yo, k2tog, p7, k2, yo, k2tog, k1, sm, k2, bring yarn between needles to front, slip last 3 sts.
Row 7 K5, sm, k3, yo, k2tog, k1, [k2tog, yo] twice, k4, yo, k2tog, [yo, k1] twice, k6—31 sts (26 sts in lace border, 5 sts in body).
Row 8 Bind off 8 (1 st on right needle when bind-off complete), k3, yo, k2tog, p7, k2, yo, k2tog, k1, remove marker, k2, p3—23 sts (18 sts in lace border, 5 sts in body).
Bind off.

FINISHING
Weave in loose ends. Block to finished measurements.•

lace-trimmed shawl

Intermediate

MATERIALS

Yarn
RED HEART® Unforgettable™, 3½oz/100g balls, each approx 280yd/256m (acrylic)
• 3 balls in 3944 Bistro

Needles
• One size 8 (5mm) circular needle, 32"/80cm, *or size to obtain gauge*

Notions
• Stitch marker
• Yarn needle

FINISHED MEASUREMENTS
Width (along top edge) 64"/162.5cm
Length (along center back) 24"/61cm

GAUGE
14 sts = 4"/10cm; 28 rows = 4"/10cm in garter st using size 8 (5mm) needle.
CHECK YOUR GAUGE. Use any size needle to obtain the gauge.

NOTES
1) The top I-cord edge (3 slipped stitches at end of Wrong Side rows), body, and lace border are all worked at the same time.
2) When slipping stitches, slip as if to knit and hold yarn to the front (Wrong Side) of the piece.
3) Shawl is worked back and forth in rows. Circular needle is used to accommodate large number of stitches. Do *not* join.
4) When adding a new ball of yarn, add it at the end of a Wrong Side row before slipping the last 3 stitches. The yarn ends can be thread down through the I-cord top edging for neat finishing.
5) Shawl can be worked from written instructions or charts.

SHAWL
Cast on 23 sts.
Set-Up Row (Wrong Side) K6, p7, k5 (for lace border), pm, k2 (for body of Shawl), bring yarn between needles to front, slip last 3 sts (for I-cord top edging).
Row 1 (Right Side) K4, yo, k1, sm, k3, yo, k2tog, k2, k2tog, yo, k5, yo, k2tog, [yo, k1] twice—26 sts (20 sts in lace border, 6 sts in body including the 3 top edging sts).
Row 2 K6, yo, k2tog, p7, k2, yo, k2tog, k1, sm, k3, bring yarn between needles to front, slip last 3 sts.
Row 3 K6, sm, k3, yo, k2tog, k1, [k2tog, yo] twice, k4, yo, k2tog, [yo, k1] twice, k2—28 sts (22 sts in lace border, 6 sts in body).
Row 4 K8, yo, k2tog, p7, k2, yo, k2tog, k1, sm, k3, bring yarn between needles to front, slip last 3 sts.
Row 5 K5, yo, k1, sm, k3, yo, k2tog, [k2tog, yo] 3 times, k3, yo, k2tog, [yo, k1] twice, k4—31 sts (24 sts in lace border, 7 sts in body).
Row 6 K10, yo, k2tog, p7, k2, yo, k2tog, k1, sm, k4, bring yarn between needles to front, slip last 3 sts.
Row 7 K7, sm, k3, yo, k2tog, k1, [k2tog, yo] twice, k4, yo, k2tog, [yo, k1] twice, k6—33 sts (26 sts in lace border, 7 sts in body).
Row 8 Bind off 8 sts (1 st on right needle when bind-off complete), k3, yo, k2tog, p7, k2, yo, k2tog, k1, sm, k4, bring yarn between needles to front, slip last 3 sts—25 sts (18 sts in lace border, 7 sts in body).

Increase Section
Row 9 (Right Side) K to 1 st before marker, yo, k1, sm, k3, yo, k2tog, k2, k2tog, yo, k5, yo, k2tog, [yo, k1] twice—28 sts (20 sts in lace border, 8 sts in body including the 3 top edging sts).
Row 10 K6, yo, k2tog, p7, k2, yo, k2tog, k1, sm, k to last 3 sts, bring yarn between needles to front, slip last 3 sts.
Row 11 K to marker, sm, k3, yo, k2tog, k1, [k2tog, yo] twice, k4, yo, k2tog, [yo, k1] twice, k2—30 sts (22 sts in lace border, 8 sts in body).
Row 12 K8, yo, k2tog, p7, k2, yo, k2tog, k1, sm, k to last 3 sts, bring yarn between needles to front, slip last 3 sts.
Row 13 K to one st before marker, yo, k1, sm, k3, yo, k2tog, [k2tog, yo] 3 times, k3, yo, k2tog, [yo, k1] twice, k4—33 sts (24 sts in lace border, 9 sts in body).

kate's shawl

Intermediate

MATERIALS

Yarn
RED HEART® Soft®, 5oz/140g balls, each approx 256yd/234m (acrylic)
• 4 balls in 9523 Dark Leaf

Needles
• One size 8 (5mm) circular needle, 32"/81cm long, or size to obtain gauge

Notions
• Stitch markers
• Removable stitch markers (optional)
• Yarn needle

FINISHED MEASUREMENTS

Width (top edge) 62"/157cm
Length (at longest point) 31"/78.5cm
Note Ruffle adds 5"/12.5cm to length and width

GAUGE

19 sts = 4"/10cm; 19 rows = 4"/10cm in Pattern Stitch using size 8 (5mm) needle. *CHECK YOUR GAUGE. Use any size needle to obtain the gauge.*

NOTES

1) Shawl is worked back and forth in rows. Circular needle is used to accommodate large number of stitches. Do *not* join.
2) Ruffle is worked in two pieces to keep the number of stitches on needle from becoming difficult to manage.

PATTERN STITCH

(multiple of 4 sts)
Row 1 (Right Side) *K1, slip 1, k1, yo, pass slipped st over both knit st and yo, k1; repeat from * across.
Row 2 Purl.
Repeat Rows 1 and 2 for Pattern Stitch.

SHAWL

Beginning at bottom point, cast on 5 sts.
Purl 1 row.
Row 1 (Right Side) K2, yo, k1, yo, k2—7 sts.
Row 2 Purl.
Row 3 K2, yo, k to last 2 sts, yo, k2—9 sts.
Row 4 Purl.
Row 5 K2, yo, k2, yo, pm, k1, pm, yo, k2, yo, k2—13 sts.
Row 6 Purl.
Note The next four rows establish the pattern. Each Right Side row will begin K2, yo and end yo, k2. It may be helpful to mark the beginning and end of the first and last complete pattern repeats on each side of the marked center stitch using removable stitch markers.
Row 7 K2, yo, work Row 1 of Pattern Stitch to first marker, yo, sm, k1, sm, yo, work Row 1 of Pattern Stitch to last 2 sts, yo, k2—17 sts.
Row 8 Purl.
Row 9 K2, yo, work Row 1 of Pattern Stitch to 2 sts before first marker, k2, yo, sm, k1, sm, yo, k2, work Row 1 of Pattern Stitch to last 2 sts, yo, k2—21 sts.
Row 10 Purl.
Repeat Rows 7–10 until there are 285 sts on needle, ending with a Wrong Side row. Bind off loosely, leaving last st on needle.

Bottom Ruffle
With Right Side facing and beginning at top left corner of shawl with remaining st on needle, pick up and k 144 stitches across left edge to bottom point (145 sts on needle), pm, pick up and k 1 stitch in point, pm, pick up and k 145 sts across right edge of shawl, ending at top right corner— 291 sts.
Row 1 (Wrong Side) P1, *yo, p1; repeat from * across—581 sts.
Row 2 K to first marker, yo, sm, k1, sm, yo, k to end—583 sts.
Row 3 Purl.
Repeat Rows 2 and 3 three more times.
Bind off loosely, leaving last st on needle.

Top Ruffle
With Right Side facing and beginning at top right edge with remaining st on needle, pick up and k 8 sts across right side edge of Bottom Ruffle (9 sts on needle), pick up and k 285 sts across top edge of shawl to top left corner of shawl, pick up and k 9 sts across left side edge of Bottom Ruffle—303 sts.
Row 1 (Wrong Side) P1, *yo, p1; repeat from * across—605 sts.
Beginning with a knit row (Right Side), work 8 more rows in Stockinette st (knit on Right Side, purl on Wrong Side). Bind off loosely.

FINISHING

Weave in loose ends. Block to finished measurements.•

pocketed scarf

Easy

MATERIALS
Yarn
RED HEART® Soft Essentials™, 5oz/141g balls, each approx 131yd/120m (acrylic) 5
- 6 balls in 7340 Cocoa

Needles
- One pair size 10 (6mm) needles, *or size to obtain gauge*

Notions
- One size J-10 (6mm) crochet hook
- Yarn needle

FINISHED MASUREMENTS
Width 15½"/39cm
Length (excluding fringe) 84"/213cm
Pocket 6"/15cm (wide) x 8"/20cm (tall)

GAUGE
14 sts = 4"/10cm; 20 rows = 4"/10cm in St st using size 10 (6mm) needles.
CHECK YOUR GAUGE. Use any size needle to obtain the gauge.

GARTER BAND PATTERN
Row 1 (Right Side) Knit.
Row 2 Purl.
Rows 3–10 Repeat Rows 1 and 2 four times more.
Row 11 (Right Side) Purl.
Row 12 (Wrong Side) Knit.
Rows 13 and 14 Repeat Rows 11 and 12.
Repeat Rows 1–14 for Garter Band Pattern.

SCARF
Cast on 53 sts.
Row 1 (Right Side) Purl.
Row 2 Knit.
Row 3 Purl.
Row 4 Knit.
Beginning with Row 1 of Garter Band Pattern, repeat Rows 1–14 for 84"/213cm, ending on Row 14.
Bind off all sts.

Pockets (make 2)
Cast on 23 sts.
Row 1 (Right Side) Knit.
Row 2 Purl.
Repeat Rows 1 and 2 for 8"/20cm.
Bind off all sts.

FINISHING
Weave in loose ends. Block to finished measurements

Attach Pockets
With Right Sides of pockets facing, place pockets on Right Side of scarf approx 11"/28cm up from bottom edge of scarf and 4¾"/12cm in from each side edge. Sew pockets in place.

Fringe
Cut sixty 16"/41cm strands of yarn. Holding 2 strands of yarn together for each fringe, use a crochet hook to evenly space each piece of fringe 1"/2.5cm apart along cast-on edge and bound-off edge of scarf—15 fringe on each end of scarf. Trim fringe.●

chevron scarf

Easy

MATERIALS

Yarn
RED HEART® With Love® Stripes™,
5oz/141g skeins, each approx
223yd/204m (acrylic)
- 2 skeins in 1978 Baroque Stripes

Needles
- One pair size 9 (5.5mm) needles, *or size to obtain gauge*

Notions
- Yarn needle

FINISHED MEASUREMENTS
Width 8"/20cm
Length 70"/178cm

GAUGE
17 sts = 4"/10cm; 20 rows = 4"/10cm in St st using size 9 (5.5mm) needles.
CHECK YOUR GAUGE. Use any size needles to obtain the gauge.

SCARF
Using long-tail cast-on, cast on 34 sts.
Row 1 (Wrong Side) K1, p to last st, K1.
Row 2 K1, kfb, k5, SKP, k2tog, K5, [kfb] twice, k5, SKP, k2tog, k5, kfb, k1.
Repeat Rows 1 and 2 until piece measures 70"/178cm.
Bind off all stitches.

FINISHING
Weave in loose ends. Block to finished measurements.•

sideways cable shawl

Intermediate

MATERIALS

Yarn
RED HEART® With Love®, 7oz/198g skeins, each approx 370yd/338m (acrylic)
- 2 skeins in 1907 Boysenberry

Needles
- One circular needle size 7 (4.5mm), 32"/81cm long, or size to obtain gauge

Notions
- Stitch markers
- Cable needle
- Yarn needle

FINISHED MEASUREMENTS
Width (along top edge) 67"/170cm
Length (at longest point) 31"/79cm

GAUGE
16 sts = 4"/10cm; 29 rows = 4"/10cm in Garter st using size 7 (4.5mm) needle.
CHECK YOUR GAUGE. Use any size needle to obtain the gauge.

NOTE
Shawl is worked back and forth in rows. Circular needle is used to accommodate large number of stitches. Do *not* join.

SPECIAL STITCH
C16B (Cable 16 Back) Slip 8 stitches to cable needle, hold to back of work, work 8 stitches from left hand needle (in pattern), work 8 stitches from cable needle (in pattern).

WRAP
Cast on 20 sts.

Increase Side
Row 1 (Right Side) Slip 1 with yarn in front, move yarn to back, k3, pm, [k2, p2] 4 times.
Row 2 K1, M1, k1, p2, [k2, p2] 3 times, sm, k4.
Row 3 Slip 1 with yarn in front, move yarn to back, k3, sm, [k2, p2] 4 times, pm, k1.
Row 4 K1, M1, sm, [k2, p2] 4 times, sm, k4.
Row 5 Slip 1 with yarn in front, move yarn to back, k3, sm, [k2, p2] 4 times, sm, k to end.
Row 6 K1, M1, k1, sm, [k2, p2] 4 times, sm, k4.
Rows 7–11 Continue in this pattern increasing one stitch (M1) on every even-numbered row, then working the increase stitch on the odd-numbered rows.
Row 12 (Wrong Side Cable Row) K1, M1, k to marker, sm, C16B, sm, k to end.

Continue working in this manner increasing one stitch (M1) at the beginning of every Wrong Side row, and working the Cable Row (C16B) every 12 rows until piece measures 31"/78cm across from cable edge to the point of the triangle or to desired length.

Decrease Side
Row 1 (Right Side) Slip 1 with yarn in front, move yarn to back, k3, sm, [k2, p2] 4 times, sm, k to last 3 stitches, k2tog, k1.
Row 2 K to marker, sm, [k2, p2] 4 times, sm, k4.
Decrease one stitch (k2tog) at end of every Right Side row, continuing to work Cable Row (C16B) every 12 rows, until 20 sts remaining. Bind off all stitches.

FINISHING
Weave in loose ends. Lightly block to finished measurements.•

everlasting super scarf

Easy

MATERIALS

Yarn
RED HEART® Grande™, 5.29oz/150g balls, each approx 46yd/42m (acrylic/wool) (7)
- 6 balls in 511 Wintergreen

Needles
- One pair size 19 (15mm) needles, *or size to obtain gauge*

FINISHED MEASUREMENTS
Width 10"/25.5cm
Length 96"/244cm

GAUGE
6 sts = 4"/10cm; 10 rows = 4"/10cm in Ridged Stitch using size 19 (15mm) needles.
CHECK YOUR GAUGE. Use any size needles to obtain the gauge.

RIDGED STITCH
(multiple of 4 sts plus 2)
Row 1 (Wrong Side) Knit.
Row 2 Knit.
Row 3 K2, *p2, k2; repeat from * to end.
Row 4 P2, *k2, p2; repeat from * to end.
Repeat Rows 1–4 for Ridged Stitch.

SCARF
Cast on 16 sts.
Knit 2 rows.
Row 1 (Wrong Side) K1 (edge st), beginning with Row 1, work Ridged Stitch over center 14 sts, k1 (edge st).
Keeping first and last st in Garter st (knit every row) and center 14 sts in Ridged Stitch, work until piece measures 95"/241cm from beginning, ending with Row 2 of Ridged Stitch.
Knit 2 rows.
Bind off knitwise.

FINISHING
Weave in loose ends. Block to finished measurements.•

garter drop-stitch scarf

Easy

MATERIALS

Yarn
RED HEART® With Love®, 7oz/198g skeins, each approx 370yd/338m (acrylic)
• 1 skein in 1252 Mango

Needles
• One pair size 9 (5.5mm) needles, *or size to obtain gauge*

FINISHED MEASUREMENTS
Width 7"/18cm
Length 60"/151cm

GAUGE
26 sts = 7"/18cm; 24 rows = 4"/10cm in Garter Stitch Wrap Pattern using size 9 (5.5mm) needles.
CHECK YOUR GAUGE. Use any size needle to obtain the gauge.

NOTE
Lightly pull the scarf in a downward motion when you finish a row. This will open and straighten the wrapped sts that you have dropped off the needle.

SCARF
Cast on 26 sts.
Rows 1–4 Knit.
Row 5 K1, wrapping yarn around needle 2 times, *K1, wrapping yarn around needle 2 times; repeat from * to last st, K1.
Row 6 Knit, dropping the wrapped sts off needle.
Repeat Rows 1–6 for Garter Stitch Wrap Pattern until scarf measures 59½"/152cm from beginning.
Rep rows 1–3 once more.
Bind off all stitches loosely.

FINISHING
Weave in loose ends. Block to finished measurements.•

boatneck poncho

Easy

MATERIALS
Yarn
RED HEART® Evermore™, 3½oz/100g balls, each approx 89yd/81m (acrylic/wool)
• 8 (9, 10, 11, 12) balls in 9938 Keepsake

Needles
• One pair size 13 (9mm) needles, *or size to obtain gauge*

Notions
• Yarn needle

SIZES
Small (Medium, Large, X-Large, XX-Large).

FINISHED MEASUREMENTS
To fit bust 32–34 (36–38, 40–42, 44–46, 48–50)"/81.5–86.5 (91.5–96.5, 101.5–106.5, 112–117, 122–127)cm
Width 40 (42, 44, 46, 48)"/101.5 (106.5, 112, 117, 122)cm
Length 20 (21½, 22, 23½, 24½)"/51 (54.5, 56, 59.5, 62)cm

GAUGE
11 sts = 4"/10cm; 14 rows = 4"/10cm in pattern using size 13 (9mm) needles.
CHECK YOUR GAUGE. Use any size needle to obtain the gauge.

NOTES
1) Each poncho panel is worked from side to side, then sewn together.
2) To accommodate the fabric width, you may prefer working back and forth in rows on a circular needle. Do *not* join.

PONCHO
Panels (make 2)
Cast on 58 (62, 66, 70, 74) sts.
Row 1 Knit.
Row 2 (Right Side) K2, yo, k2tog, *k2, k into the back of next st, p1; repeat from * to last 6 sts, k2, k2tog, yo, k2.
Row 3 K2, p2, *k2, k into the back of next st, p1; repeat from * to last 6 sts, k2, p2, k2.
Repeat Rows 2 and 3 until piece measures 39½ (41½, 43½, 45½, 47½)"/100.5 (105.5, 110.5, 115.5, 120.5)cm from cast-on edge, ending with Row 2.
Next row (Wrong Side) Knit.
Bind off all stitches as if to knit.

FINISHING
With yarn needle and Wrong Sides of panels held together, sew shoulder seams across one long edge as follows:
Begin first shoulder seam at a top corner and sew for about 15 (16, 16½, 17½, 18)"/38 (40.5, 42, 44.5, 45.5)cm. Repeat on opposite shoulder seam, leaving center 10 (10, 11, 11, 12)"/25.5 (25.5, 28, 28, 30.5)cm open for neck. With yarn needle, tack lower corners together to form sleeve. Weave in loose ends.•

fall berries shawl

Easy

MATERIALS
Yarn
RED HEART® Soft®, 5oz/141g balls, each approx 256yd/234m (acrylic) (4)
- 3 balls in 9263 Cinnabar

Needles
- One size 9 (5.5mm) circular needle, 32"/81cm, *or size to obtain gauge*

Notions
- Removable stitch marker
- Yarn needle

GAUGE
26 sts = 4"/10cm; 21 rows = 4"/10cm in Bramble St using 9 (5.5mm) needle. *CHECK YOUR GAUGE. Use any size needle to obtain the gauge.*

FINISHED MEASUREMENTS
Width (along widest edge) 63"/160cm
Length 23"/58.5cm

SPECIAL STITCHES
kfbf (knit into front, back, and front)
Knit next st but do not remove from needle, knit into back loop of same st and then into the front of the same st again; remove from needle—2 sts increased.

NOTES
1) Slip stitches purlwise.
2) Circular needle is used to accommodate large number of stitches. Do *not* join.

BRAMBLE STITCH
(multiple of 4 sts)
Row 1 (Right Side) *(K1, p1, k1) all in the same stitch, p3tog; repeat from * across.
Row 2 Purl.
Row 3 *P3tog, (k1, p1, k1) all in the same stitch; repeat from * across.
Row 4 Purl.
Repeat Rows 1–4 for Bramble St.

SHAWL
Cast on 1 stitch.
Row 1 (Right Side) Kfbf—3 sts.
Rows 2, 4, and 6 Purl.
Row 3 Slip 1, kfb, k to end—4 sts.
Row 5 Repeat Row 3—5 sts.
Row 7 Repeat Row 3—6 sts.
Row 8 Purl.

Begin Bramble Stitch
Row 1 (Right Side) Sl 1, kfb, pm, (k1, p1, k1) all in the same stitch, p3tog—1 st increased.
Row 2 and all Wrong Side rows Purl.
Row 3 Sl 1, kfb, k to marker, sm, p3tog, (k1, p1, k1) all in the same stitch—1 st increased.
Row 5 Sl 1, kfb, k to marker, sm, (k1, p1, k1) all in the same stitch, p3tog—1 st increased.
Row 7 Repeat Row 3—1 st increased.
Row 9 Repeat Row 5—1 st increased.
Row 11 Sl 1, kfb, k1, remove marker and replace after these 4 sts, sm, [p3tog, (k1, p1, k1) all in the same stitch] to end of row—1 st increased.
Rows 13 and 17 Sl 1, kfb, k to marker, sm, [(k1, p1, k1) all in the same stitch, p3tog] to end of row—1 st increased.
Row 15 Sl 1, kfb, k to marker, sm, [p3tog, (k1, p1, k1) all in the same stitch] to end of row—1 st increased.
Row 18 Purl.
Repeat Rows 11–18 thirty-three times or until shawl is desired size.
Work Row 11, once more.
Bind off all stitches.

FINISHING
Weave in loose ends. Block to finished measurements.

Optional Tassles (Make 3)
Cut one 12"/30.5cm and twenty-five 8"/10cm strands of yarn.
Put all 8"/10cm strands together and tie in center with the 12"/30.5cm strand. Fold 8"/10cm strands down over tie and tie again with 12"/30.5 strand, about 1"/2.5cm down from fold.
Trim tassel, if necessary.
Sew a tassel to each point of the shawl.•

cable-edged scarf

Easy

MATERIALS

Yarn
RED HEART® Soft®, 5oz/141g balls, each approx 256yd/234m (acrylic)
- 2 balls in 2515 Turquoise

Needles
- One pair size 8 (5mm) needles, *or size to obtain gauge*

Notions
- Stitch markers
- Cable needle
- Yarn needle

FINISHED MEASUREMENTS

Width 6"/15cm
Length 60"/152cm

GAUGE

18 sts = 4"/10cm; 28 rows = 4"/10cm in garter st using size 8 (5mm) needles.
CHECK YOUR GAUGE. Use any size needles to obtain the gauge.

1x1 RIB

(over an odd number of sts)
Row 1 (Right Side) *K1, p1; repeat from * to last st, k1.
Row 2 *P1, k1; repeat from * to last st, p1.
Repeat Rows 1 and 2 for 1x1 Rib.

BRAID CABLE

(worked over 12 sts)
Row 1 (Right Side) Knit.
Row 2 Purl.
Row 3 Slip 4 sts to cable needle and hold in back, k4, k4 from cable needle, k4.
Rows 4, 6, and 8 Purl.
Rows 5 and 7 Knit.
Row 9 K4, slip 4 sts to cable needle and hold in front, k4, k4 from cable needle.
Row 10 Purl.
Row 11 Knit.
Row 12 Purl.
Repeat Rows 1–12 for Braid Cable.

SCARF

Cast on 41 sts. Work in 1x1 rib for 12 rows, decrease 6 sts evenly on last row—35 sts.
Row 1 (Right Side) K1, pm, work Row 1 of Braid Cable, pm, k9, pm, work Row 1 of Braid Cable, pm, k1.
Row 2 K1, sm, work Row 2 of Braid Cable, sm, k9, sm, work Row 1 of Braid Cable, sm, k1.
Continue in pattern until piece measures 58"/147.5cm, ending with Row 11 of Braid Cable. Work in 1x1 rib for 12 rows, increase 6 sts evenly on first row—41 sts.
Bind off all sts.

FINISHING

Weave in loose ends. Block to finished measurements.•

Row 62 K1, kfb, k to marker, yo, sm, k2, sm, yo, k to last 3 sts, kfb, k2—132 sts.
Rows 63 and 65 K to marker, sm, p2, sm, k to end.
Row 64 K1, kfb, k to marker, yo, sm, k2, sm, yo, k to last 3 sts, kfb, k2—136 sts.
Rows 66, 68, 70, and 72 K1, kfb, k to marker, yo, sm, k2, sm, yo, k to last 3 sts, kfb, k2—152 sts on last row worked.
Rows 67, 69, and 71 K2, p to last 2 sts, k2.

Section Four
Row 73 (Wrong Side) K to marker, sm, p2, sm, k to end.
Row 74 K1, kfb, k to marker, yo, sm, k2, sm, yo, k to last 3 sts, kfb, k2—156 sts.
Row 75 K to marker, sm, p2, sm, k to end.
Row 76 K1, kfb, k to marker, yo, sm, k2, sm, yo, k to last 3 sts, kfb, k2—160 sts.
Row 77 K2, p1, [yo, p2tog] to marker, sm, p2, sm, [p2tog, yo] to last 3 sts, p1, k2.
Row 78 K1, kfb, k to marker, yo, sm, k2, sm, yo, k to last 3 sts, kfb, k2—164 sts.
Repeat Rows 75–78 four more times—196 sts on last row worked.
Row 95 (Wrong Side) Knit.
Row 96 K1, kfb, k to marker, yo, sm, k2, sm, yo, k to last 3 sts, kfb, k2—200 sts.
Row 97 Knit.
Bind off loosely knitwise.

FINISHING
Weave in loose ends. If needed, block to finished measurements by spraying with water and allowing shawl to dry.•

textured triangle shawl

Easy

MATERIALS
Yarn
RED HEART® Chunky Soft™, 5oz/141g balls, each approx 131yd/120m (acrylic) (5)
• 3 balls in 7420 Charcoal

Needles
• One size 11 (8mm) circular needle, 29"/74cm long, *or size to obtain gauge*

Notions
• Stitch markers
• Yarn needle

FINISHED MEASUREMENTS
Width (at widest point) 70"/178cm
Length (at longest point) 30"/76cm

GAUGE
10 sts = 4"/10cm; 16 rows = 4"10cm in St st using size 11 (8mm) needle.
CHECK YOUR GAUGE. Use any size needles to obtain the gauge.

NOTES
1) Shawl is worked back and forth in rows. Circular needle is used to accommodate large number of stitches. Do *not* join.
2) Bind off loosely. You may choose to use a needle size one or two sizes larger.

SHAWL
Garter Tab
Cast on 2 sts.
Knit 8 rows (4 garter ridges). Do *not* turn after last row.
Pick up and knit 4 sts along edges of row, one for each garter st ridge, then pick up and knit 2 sts along cast-on edge—8 sts.

Set Up Rows
Row 1 (Wrong Side) K2, p to last 2 sts, k2.
Row 2 K1, kfb, k1, yo, pm, k2, pm, yo, kfb, k2—12 sts.
Row 3 K2, p to last 2 sts, k2.

Section One
Row 4 (Right Side) K1, kfb, k to marker, yo, sm, k2, sm, yo, k to last 3 sts, kfb, k2—16 sts; 4 sts increased.
Row 5 K2, p to last 2 sts, k2.
Repeat last 2 rows 13 more times and then Row 4 once more—72 sts on last row worked.

Section Two
Row 33 (Wrong Side) K to marker, sm, p2, sm, k to end.
Row 34 K1, kfb, k to marker, yo, sm, k2, sm, yo, k to last 3 sts, kfb, k2—76 sts.
Row 35 K to marker, sm, p2, sm, k to end.
Row 36 K1, kfb, k to marker, yo, sm, k2, sm, yo, k to last 3 sts, kfb, k2—80 sts.
Row 37 K2, p1, [yo, p2tog] to marker, sm, p2, sm, [p2tog, yo] to last 3 sts, p1, k2.
Row 38 K1, kfb, k to marker, yo, sm, k2, sm, yo, k to last 3 sts, kfb, k2—84 sts.
Repeat Rows 35–38 two more times, then Rows 33–35 once—104 sts on last row worked.

Section Three
Rows 50, 52, 54, and 56 (Right Side) K1, kfb, k to marker, yo, sm, k2, sm, yo, k to last 3 sts, kfb, k2—120 sts on last row worked.
Rows 51, 53, and 55 K2, p to last 2 sts, k2.
Row 57 K to marker, sm, p2, sm, k to end.
Row 58 K1, kfb, k to marker, yo, sm, k2, sm, yo, k to last 3 sts, kfb, k2—124 sts.
Row 59 K to marker, sm, p2, sm, k to end.
Row 60 K1, kfb, k to marker, yo, sm, k2, sm, yo, k to last 3 sts, kfb, k2—128 sts.
Row 61 K2, p1, [yo, p2tog] to marker, sm, p2, sm, [p2tog, yo] to last 3 sts, p1, k2.

content

Page 46

Page 28

Page 11

Page 26

Page 24

Page 42

Page 30

Page 18

Page 40

Page 36

Page 38

Page 34

- 2 Textured Triangle Shawl
- 4 Cable-Edged Scarf
- 6 Fall Berries Shawl
- 8 Boatneck Poncho
- 10 Garter Drop-Stitch Scarf
- 11 Everlasting Super Scarf
- 12 Sideways Cable Shawl
- 14 Chevron Scarf
- 16 Pocketed Scarf
- 18 Kate's Shawl
- 20 Lace-Trimmed Shawl
- 24 Laid-Back Shawl
- 26 Reverse Sand Stitch Scarf
- 28 Cozy Shoulders Poncho
- 30 Crescent Shawl
- 32 Lacy Ridges Shawl
- 34 Honeycomb Stitch Scarf
- 35 Eight-Hour Shawl
- 36 Statement Scarf
- 38 Zigzaggy Scarf
- 40 Voyager Poncho
- 42 Ribbed Slit Shawl
- 44 Stunning Lace Scarf
- 46 Brighten My Day Shawl
- 48 Lacy Stripes Scarf